Take Back Control

Reclaiming Your Privacy in the Digital Age

By:

V. Pathak

ISBN: 978-93-343-6124-7

Published under the independent imprint of V. Pathak, India.

Printed in India | July 2025

Acknowledgements

For the Ones Who Made Privacy Personal

This book didn't happen in isolation—neither does privacy.

It was shaped, challenged, and sharpened by people who understand that protecting privacy is not just a technical issue, but a deeply human one.

First, thank you to the countless individuals whose real-world experiences informed these pages. The stories of parents who lost their peace of mind to identity theft, travelers whose devices were searched without cause, workers monitored without their knowledge—your experiences are what turned theory into urgency.

To the privacy advocates, cybersecurity researchers, open-source developers, and digital rights defenders: your work laid the foundation. Whether you built a tracker blocker, exposed unethical surveillance, or gave a voice to those overlooked—this book stands on your shoulders.

A special thanks to those who took the time to educate others when it wasn't easy or convenient—to the teachers, bloggers, podcasters, and friends who patiently explained how encryption works or why it matters who reads your data. You're the unsung heroes of the privacy movement.

To the engineers and designers creating tools that protect without needing technical degrees to use—thank you for proving that privacy can be both powerful and simple.

To my early readers and critics who didn't just nod along but asked the hard questions, flagged blind spots, and made sure every chapter earned its place—your honesty made this stronger.

To my family and close friends: thank you for understanding when I went quiet to write, for letting me test every tool on your phones, and for reminding me why this fight matters—because privacy is not just about principle, it's about protecting the people we love.

And finally, to you—the reader.

You took the time to learn, reflect, and act.

You cared enough to question the default.

You proved that privacy is not dead. It's just waiting for people like you to defend it.

Thank you for taking this journey.

Now go help someone else take theirs.

Content

Part I

Personal Life (Home and Online)

Understanding Your Digital Footprint and Securing Your Private Life

It Started with a School Form

Meera thought nothing of it when she filled out a school admission form for her son. Name, address, Aadhaar number, parents' occupations—routine details. Two weeks later, she received a call from her bank. Someone had opened a credit card in her name. Another call followed. A loan application had been filed using her husband's identity.

A data breach had exposed their personal information. That simple school form, stored on an unsecured server, became the gateway to financial chaos. By the time they noticed, the damage was done: ₹3.5 lakhs in unauthorized transactions, several hours of police reports, and a hit to their credit score.

What happened to Meera's family isn't rare. It's happening every day.

You Are Not Invisible

Every tap, swipe, voice command, and "agree to terms" creates a digital trail. Whether you're ordering groceries, googling a health question, or using a smart speaker to play music—you're feeding a vast network of data collectors.

And most of us never even pause to ask:

Who's watching? Who's storing that data? Who's profiting from it? And what are they doing with it?

The truth is, you don't need to be "doing something wrong" to be surveilled. You just need to exist online.

The Illusion of Control

We like to believe we're in control—setting a phone passcode, turning off "location tracking," maybe switching to Incognito mode. But here's the uncomfortable truth: those are speed bumps, not barriers. Your apps still collect data. Your browser still logs searches. Your location is still triangulated through cell towers even if GPS is off.

You don't control your data. You lease it.

And the lease terms? Buried in 10,000-word privacy policies nobody reads.

The Unseen Web of Exposure

Let's bring this home with some numbers:

- 18 million people in the U.S. were victims of identity fraud in 2024.
- ₹1,400 crore lost to online scams in India last year alone.
- A single shopping app may contain over 50 embedded trackers, many sending data to unknown third parties.

It's not just identity theft. It's targeted advertising that knows you better than your partner. It's predictive algorithms that manipulate your behavior. It's smart devices listening in when they shouldn't.

Still think you're just an anonymous user in the system?

It Could Happen to You

Nikhil, a 28-year-old engineer in Bengaluru, didn't think much about privacy. He had the latest Android phone, a few lifestyle apps, and was always connected. One morning, he noticed strange messages on his screen—his Google account was logged in from an IP in Russia. A few hours later, his LinkedIn profile was spammed with fake job postings. Days later, someone used his digital wallet to book flight tickets.

He had reused the same password on 14 different services. One data breach leaked it all.

His story isn't about ignorance—it's about how even the smart, tech-savvy ones get caught off guard.

What This Part Will Help You Do

This first part of the book is your foundation.

You'll:

- Understand what makes up your digital footprint and where your information leaks from.
- Learn how social media, smartphones, and even smart homes silently collect and share your private details.
- Discover practical steps to reclaim your privacy—without needing a tech degree.

Think of it like learning how to lock your front door—but for your digital life.

You wouldn't leave your house open while you sleep. Why leave your data exposed 24/7?

Why Now, Why You

A recent survey showed that 59% of people admit they don't know what companies do with their data. And 72% feel they've "lost control" over their personal information.

This book exists to change that.

It doesn't matter if you're a college student, a working mom, a retired accountant, or a tech startup founder. If you use the internet—and let's be real, you do—this is your fight.

And it's one you can win.

The Promise

You're not powerless. You don't have to be paranoid. And you don't have to quit the internet or throw away your phone.

What you do need is awareness, action, and a clear roadmap.

That's what you'll find here: no jargon, no fear-mongering, no guilt-tripping. Just clarity, simplicity, and practical advice.

Let's start by mapping your footprint.

Chapter 1

Privacy Wake-Up Call

Stories from the Digital Frontlines

The School Form That Unleashed Chaos

On a muggy September morning in Mumbai, Rachna Mehta stood in her bank's customer service queue, sweating—not from the heat, but from panic. A letter had arrived the night before. It was a credit card bill for an account she never opened. ₹1.2 lakhs in charges. Electronics, hotel bookings, even a gold chain. All billed to her name.

She hadn't applied for any card.

By noon, she learned her PAN number had been used to open two credit lines, a third was pending, and a new SIM card in her name had been activated in a different city.

Rachna is a schoolteacher. Her husband is a structural engineer. Their son, Arnav, had just started fifth grade. Three months earlier, she filled out a digital admission form on the school's website—standard stuff: names, addresses, Aadhaar numbers, parents' jobs, and yes, PAN numbers for fee processing.

That form was stored on an unsecured server. A school database was breached—quietly, without any public announcement. The attackers didn't deface the site. They siphoned off thousands of student-family records and sold them on the dark web.

Rachna's nightmare had begun with a routine form. By the time she learned what had happened, her credit score had tanked, her savings were locked in fraud investigations, and she was spending weekends filing police complaints instead of tutoring her son.

The App That Turned a Routine into a Trap

In another city, another person was living through a quieter violation.

Tanvi Rawat, a 26-year-old graphic designer in Pune, lived alone and kept a strict daily routine. She left for work at 9:00 a.m., grabbed coffee at the same corner café, and returned home around 7:30 p.m. She used a popular weather app—free, sleek, and accurate. It asked for location access. She said yes, as most people do.

Months passed. She noticed a man often sitting near her café. Then at the metro station. Then outside her apartment block. She brushed it off until he smiled at her one day and said, "You're late today." She hadn't posted her schedule online. She hadn't shared it with anyone.

Shaken, she contacted a friend in cybersecurity who examined her phone. That free weather app had been collecting her location in the background every five minutes. Worse, it was selling the data to third-party brokers. The brokers resold it—to marketers, analytics firms, and potentially anyone willing to pay.

Tanvi's stalker didn't need to hack her. He bought her data.

She deleted the app. She changed her routine. She moved houses. But the damage had already been done—her sense of safety, trust, and privacy had been permanently shaken.

These Aren't Rare Cases

You might think these are exceptions. They're not.

- In 2024 alone, over 18 million Americans were victims of identity fraud.
- ₹1,400 crore was lost to digital scams in India.
- A single data broker can collect and trade profiles on more than 500 million individuals, including GPS movements, shopping habits, and even emotional states inferred from app behavior.

Most people don't realize how much of their life is exposed until something bad happens. And when it does, the response is often: *"I didn't know."* But ignorance is no shield when your personal data becomes a weapon.

Why These Stories Matter?

Stories like Rachna's and Tanvi's serve a deeper purpose—they make the invisible threat real. It's easy to read about "data breaches" and "privacy policies" and feel detached. But when you see a mother drained by fraud or a young woman forced to move homes because of silent tracking, the stakes become clear.

These are not technical failures. They are systemic blind spots in a world that treats personal data like currency, and individuals like data points.

Rachna trusted a school form. Tanvi trusted an app. You probably trust dozens of websites, apps, and devices every day without thinking twice. And that's exactly what these systems rely on: your silent consent.

Your Data Has a Life of Its Own

Once your data is collected—your location, your clicks, your habits—it begins to live a life of its own. It's copied, shared, sold, categorized, and used to build digital profiles that follow you across the internet. Sometimes, even across borders.

Have you ever searched for a product on one site and seen ads for it on another? That's not coincidence. That's surveillance capitalism in action.

Now imagine if the data being shared wasn't just your shopping interest—but your health status, your income range, or your political leaning. Because that's happening, too.

The Wake-Up is Personal

This chapter isn't here to scare you—it's here to wake you up.

You don't have to become paranoid. But you do need to become aware. You need to understand:

- Where your data goes
- Who benefits from it
- How it can be misused
- And how you can reclaim control

Because privacy isn't dead. It's just quietly slipping through your fingers.

And once you understand that, you can stop the leak.

What's Coming Next?

In the chapters that follow, we'll peel back the curtain on how your data is collected, who profits from it, and—most importantly—how to fight back. You'll learn:

- How websites and apps track you (and how to block them)
- How to review and restrict app permissions
- How to use privacy settings effectively on social media
- How to protect your devices at home
- And how to develop habits that protect your digital life

This journey isn't about perfection. It's about power.

And it starts with knowing the battlefield.

Did You Know?

- 60% of Americans believe daily life is impossible without data tracking.
- Some popular "free" flashlight apps request access to your microphone, contacts, and camera.
- A single visit to a news website can trigger 30+ hidden trackers, most of which are invisible to you.

Checklist: Reality Check

Take five minutes to do this now:

- Google your full name. What shows up?
- Check your phone: Which apps have access to your location?
- Visit your social media profile (as a stranger). What can people see?

If that surprised you, you're in the right place.

You wouldn't leave your home unlocked.

You wouldn't let strangers rifle through your wallet.

So why leave your digital life wide open?

Privacy isn't a luxury—it's your right. And the more you understand it, the more you can protect it.

Chapter 2

The Data You Leave Behind

How Personal Information is Collected?

You're Leaking Data Right Now

If you're reading this on a smartphone, tablet, or computer, you're sharing information—right now. It may not feel like it. You didn't sign a form or give anyone explicit permission. But your device is already communicating with dozens of third parties.

Your screen size, battery level, location, IP address, browser version, operating system, and typing patterns are being logged in real time. That's before you even click anything.

Welcome to your digital footprint—the trail of data you leave behind every time you go online, often without realizing it.

And that trail is deep, wide, and persistent.

Everyday Data, Everywhere

Let's walk through a typical day.

- Morning: You ask your smart speaker for the weather. It logs your voice, stores the request, and may send audio clips to cloud servers "for quality improvement."
- Commuting: Your maps app tracks your route in the background, collecting real-time GPS data—even if the app isn't open.
- At work: You Google something personal on your office Wi-Fi. That search is recorded by your browser, your company's network logs, and likely Google's servers.
- During lunch: You scroll social media. Your likes, comments, watch time, and even how long you pause on a post are tracked.
- Evening: You unwind with a smart TV show. Your viewing history, pause/play behavior, and even remote control

interactions are sent back to the manufacturer or streaming provider.

By bedtime, you've generated thousands of data points. And that's just one day.

What's Being Collected?

Here's a breakdown of what's typically gathered:

Source	Data Collected
Social Media Apps	Profile info, friend lists, message metadata, behavior patterns, facial recognition tags
Search Engines	Search terms, time stamps, click history, language preferences
Smartphones	Location, contacts, microphone input, browsing history, app usage
Wearables	Heart rate, step count, sleep cycles, stress levels
Smart TVs & IoT Devices	Audio recordings, usage patterns, content preferences
Web Browsers	Cookies, session data, installed extensions, bookmarks

Each piece of data might seem harmless on its own. But when combined, it creates an eerily accurate portrait of who you are, what you do, and what you might do next.

Who's Collecting It?

You're not just sharing data with the apps and services you use. That's only the beginning.

- Tech Giants: Google, Meta (Facebook/Instagram/WhatsApp), Amazon, Apple, Microsoft. These companies collect your data to improve services, target ads, and refine algorithms.
- Advertisers: Partner networks embed trackers across websites and apps to build profiles for micro-targeting. Your behavior fuels their ad revenue.
- Data Brokers: Perhaps the most shadowy players. These are firms you've never heard of—like Acxiom, Experian, Oracle Data Cloud—who buy, merge, and sell data profiles. They compile details from public records, purchase histories, credit card transactions, and online behavior.

You never gave them your name. But they know you. And they profit from you.

Behind the Scenes: How Tracking Cookies Work

Cookies aren't just for remembering your login.

Here's what's really happening:

- You visit a news website.
- That site loads ads from multiple companies.
- Each company drops a small file (a "cookie") onto your browser.

- These cookies track your behavior across multiple sites, linking your activity to a digital ID.

Example: You read a product review on Site A. Hours later, you see ads for that product on Sites B, C, and D—even on a different device.

That's cross-site tracking.

Some cookies expire in minutes. Others live for years. Some even respawn after deletion, using fingerprinting techniques that identify you based on device configuration and browser setup.

Your Data is For Sale—Literally

Ever get a call from a real estate agent after browsing home listings once? Or an email for fertility products after Googling baby names?

You didn't opt in. You were profiled.

Data brokers aggregate information and sell it in bulk to marketers, political campaigns, insurance companies, and more. Categories may include:

- "People who live paycheck to paycheck"
- "Adults recently divorced"
- "Consumers with diabetes"
- "Young voters likely to support XYZ party"

These labels aren't guesses. They're built from thousands of data points harvested from your clicks, purchases, searches, and app behavior.

And once you're in a category, you're targeted accordingly—whether it's ads, pricing changes, or even credit decisions.

One Click, Dozens of Trackers

Let's break this down visually. When you visit a popular news site:

1. The page loads articles, banners, and videos.
2. Ad networks ping multiple servers for real-time bidding.
3. Trackers record your location, device type, browsing history, and more.
4. Some trackers are embedded invisibly through pixels or JavaScript.
5. Others are tied to your social logins (e.g. "Login with Facebook" buttons), letting those platforms monitor your behavior off-platform too.

Studies show that the average website hosts 20–30 third-party trackers. Many are undetectable without special tools.

You think you're reading news. But you're actually broadcasting your behavior to dozens of invisible watchers.

You Don't Own the Data—They Do

The apps you download often bury consent in legalese. You agree to broad data usage clauses without realizing what they authorize:

- "We may share anonymized data with third parties" (but it's often re-identifiable)
- "We collect usage and diagnostic information" (which can include location and messages metadata)
- "We use your information to improve user experience" (translation: personalize ads and retain attention)

Once your data is in their system, you can't take it back. You can ask to delete it—sometimes.

But there's no guarantee it's removed from all backups, mirrors, or partner databases.

You might leave the app. But your data often stays.

Why This Matters?

You may think: "So what? I'm not doing anything wrong."

That's not the point.

Your data can:

- Be used to influence your decisions (targeted ads, political content)
- Be sold to companies you never interacted with
- Be used to deny you opportunities (insurance, credit scoring, jobs)
- Be hacked and leaked in data breaches you never signed up for

You deserve to know where your data goes, and who profits from it. Because knowledge leads to control. And control is power.

What You Can Do Now?

Let's take your first step toward awareness.

Checklist: Map Your Footprint

- Google your name and email. What's publicly visible?
- Open your phone's settings. Review app permissions—who can access your camera, mic, and location?
- Check your browser. Are third-party cookies blocked? Install a privacy extension like uBlock Origin or Privacy Badger.

- Visit www.simpleoptout.com or www.aboutthedata.com and try to opt out from data broker lists.

You won't erase your footprint overnight. But you can start shrinking it.

Pro Tips

"Don't just install an app— audit it.

Ask: Why does this flashlight app need my location? Why does a game need access to my contacts? Less is more."

Final Thought

Your digital trail doesn't just follow you—it defines you in the eyes of companies, governments, and algorithms. It shapes what you see, what you're offered, and what's decided about you.

Understanding how that data is collected is the first step toward reclaiming your autonomy.

In the next chapter, we'll ask the next question: Who's profiting from all this—and at what cost to you?

Chapter 3

Big Brother Inc.

Who's Profiting from Your Data?

“Free” Isn’t Free

You’re scrolling through a social media app. Watching videos. Laughing at memes. Maybe posting a photo of your pet. You didn’t pay to join. There’s no subscription fee. Just a couple of ads here and there.

Seems harmless, right?

But here's the truth: If you’re not paying for the product, you are the product.

That selfie you posted? The post you liked? The article you clicked on but didn’t finish? All of it is data. That data is captured, analyzed, sorted, and sold—sometimes in real time.

The business model is simple: gather everything about you and sell access to your attention.

Your Behavior Is a Commodity

Take a moment to consider this: in 2024, Meta (Facebook, Instagram, WhatsApp) generated over $130 billion in revenue. Almost all of it came from advertising. Not product sales. Not user subscriptions. Just ads.

But these aren’t the clunky banners of the early internet. They’re hyper-targeted, algorithmically delivered, emotionally engineered messages—built on what the platform knows about you:

- Your birthday
- Your relationship status
- Your recent searches
- What you hovered over but didn’t click
- How long you watched a video

- Who you message most

This is surveillance advertising. And it's not just Meta. Google, TikTok, Snapchat, X (formerly Twitter), and even Spotify and YouTube operate on similar models.

You're not just a user. You're a data source—and that data fuels a global economy.

Enter the Data Brokers

Behind the scenes of your online life is a vast, largely invisible industry: data brokering.

These are companies you've likely never heard of— Acxiom, Oracle Data Cloud, Experian Marketing Services, CoreLogic, and hundreds of others. They don't run apps. They don't show ads. They just collect, buy, combine, and sell information.

What kind of information?

- Your full name
- Home and work address
- Shopping habits
- Travel patterns
- Marital status
- Political affiliation
- Religion
- Household income
- Health interests (like searches related to diabetes, fertility, or depression)

Some even offer categories like:

- "Anxious Moms"

- "Rural Renters with Low Credit"
- "People Likely to Buy Pet Insurance"
- "Cancer Survivors Who Donate to Political Causes"

These profiles are then sold to advertisers, insurance companies, political campaigns—even law enforcement.

You don't need to interact with a data broker for them to build a profile on you. They harvest from your credit card transactions, loyalty programs, social media behavior, public records, browser history, and apps you've installed.

Real Case: The Cambridge Analytica Scandal

One of the most infamous examples of data misuse came to light in 2018: Cambridge Analytica.

The company harvested data from over 87 million Facebook users—without their knowledge or consent—through a quiz app. While only a few hundred thousand people downloaded the app, Facebook's API allowed the developer to also collect data on their entire friend networks.

Cambridge Analytica used this trove of data to create psychographic profiles—essentially, psychological models that predicted user behavior, preferences, and vulnerabilities. These profiles were then used to deliver targeted political ads during the 2016 U.S. presidential election and the Brexit referendum.

People weren't just being marketed to—they were being manipulated.

That scandal prompted hearings, fines, and a global reckoning over data rights. But despite the outrage, the fundamental business model remains unchanged.

The Illusion of Consent

Most companies will tell you they collect data "with your consent."

But let's be honest:

- Did you read the 27-page privacy policy when you installed that app?
- Do you understand what "may share data with trusted third parties" really means?
- Were you given a genuine choice—or just "Accept" or "Exit"?

This isn't informed consent. It's coerced convenience. And it's designed that way.

The majority of users click "agree" just to move forward. In doing so, they often agree to:

- Microphone access
- Location tracking
- Third-party sharing
- Behavioral profiling
- Cross-device tracking

And once consent is given, revoking it doesn't always delete what was already taken.

Where the Laws Fall Short?

In many countries—especially the U.S.—privacy laws are patchy at best. There's no unified federal law regulating how companies collect or sell personal data.

Compare that to the European Union's GDPR (General Data Protection Regulation), which gives users:

- The right to access their data
- The right to correct inaccuracies
- The right to be forgotten
- The right to restrict processing
- The right to object to profiling

Under GDPR, companies face massive fines for non-compliance. But in the U.S., most privacy protections are industry-specific (like HIPAA for health data or COPPA for children), not universal.

This legal vacuum allows companies to exploit user data with minimal oversight.

Data as a Weapon

Let's be clear: data isn't just for selling you shoes or soft drinks.

It's used to:

- Predict voter turnout and tailor political messages
- Dynamically change prices based on what you're likely to pay
- Flag applicants as "risky" in financial or employment contexts
- Determine eligibility for housing, healthcare, or credit

- Target vulnerable populations (like people struggling with addiction or mental health)

This is where data capitalism becomes data discrimination.

And without transparency, most people don't even know it's happening.

Expert Perspective

Interview Excerpt – Asha Menon, Privacy Advocate, Digital Rights India

"Most people assume their data is safe if they aren't breaking the law. That's dangerously naïve. In reality, personal data is used to sort, judge, and influence us—often without our knowledge. The systems aren't neutral. They reflect the priorities of the companies that build them: profit, performance, and power."

She continues:

"The solution isn't to go offline. It's to demand transparency, meaningful consent, and real accountability. Until then, your data isn't yours."

What You Can Do?

You can't boycott every company. But you can start taking control.

Checklist: Privacy Profit Pushback

- Check which companies track you using https://whotracks.me
- Install tracker blockers (e.g. uBlock Origin, Privacy Badger)

- Use browsers like Brave or Firefox with privacy settings maxed
- Avoid "Login with Facebook/Google" options on new sites
- Revoke unnecessary app permissions (especially location, mic, contacts)
- Use email aliases when signing up for services
- Opt out of data brokers at https://optoutprescreen.com or https://simpleoptout.com

You won't disappear from the grid—but you'll become a lot harder to track.

Final Thought

Your data is valuable—so valuable that billion-dollar companies have built empires around harvesting and monetizing it.

They treat your personal life like a commodity. They profit from your attention, your behavior, your preferences, and even your fears.

But once you understand the game, you can start playing it on your terms.

In the next chapter, we'll focus on one of the most powerful players in the data economy: social media—and how to reclaim your digital identity in a world that profits from oversharing.

Chapter 4

Social Media and Oversharing

Protecting Your Online Identity

Connected... and Exposed

It started with a post.

Ravi had just bought a brand-new SUV. Excited, he shared a photo on Facebook—parked in his driveway, with a shiny red bow still tied to the hood.

The caption read: *"First big purchase! Can't wait for the first road trip!"* Comments and likes poured in. Friends congratulated him. Some asked for a ride.

Three days later, while Ravi and his wife were out celebrating, their home was burglarized.

The thieves knew the model of the car, his general location (visible through geo-tagging), and the fact that he wasn't home. The driveway photo gave away more than he realized: the house's layout, number plate, and neighborhood clues.

What started as a proud moment turned into a costly mistake.

What Are You Really Sharing?

Social media is built to encourage sharing. Milestones, birthdays, vacations, achievements, even losses—it's how we connect. But the platforms don't just connect people—they expose them.

Every post, comment, like, and follow creates a digital breadcrumb. Often, we share without realizing the cumulative exposure.

Let's break down common oversharing risks:

Content Shared	Potential Risk
New purchase posts	Signals financial status to scammers
Vacation announcements	Tells burglars you're not home
Kids' photos with school uniforms	Reveals location and identity
Birthdates, anniversaries	Can help guess passwords or security questions
Political opinions	Can be used for profiling or harassment
Geotags on photos	Pinpoint your real-time location

You're not just talking to friends—you're broadcasting to the world. And sometimes, the wrong people are listening.

Oversharing Fuels Social Engineering

Social engineering isn't just a fancy term. It's how scammers use your publicly available information to manipulate you.

Example: A fraudster scans your LinkedIn and Facebook profiles. He sees your mother's maiden name from a tagged family photo. He learns you bank with SBI based on a tweet you posted about your frustrating branch visit. He notices you frequently check into a local café every Monday.

That's enough for a spear phishing attack—an email that looks exactly like it came from your bank, referencing a "recent café purchase," asking you to verify a transaction.

You click. You enter your credentials. Your account gets drained.

It doesn't take hacking skills. Just observation—and your help.

Privacy Settings: Your First Line of Defense

Most social media platforms offer decent privacy controls. The problem is: few users ever tweak the defaults.

Here's what you should check—right now:

Facebook

- Limit who can see your future posts (set to "Friends" or custom lists).
- Review old posts and remove public ones.
- Disable facial recognition features.
- Restrict who can find you by phone/email.
- Turn off location history.

Instagram

- Switch to a private account.
- Remove location tags from past posts.
- Block unknown or suspicious followers.
- Disable activity status (so others can't see when you're online).
- Review third-party apps connected via Instagram login.

Twitter/X

- Protect your tweets (makes them visible only to approved followers).
- Disable location tagging in tweets.
- Turn off discoverability by email/phone number.
- Review connected apps.
- Block or mute trolls and bots.

TikTok

- Set account to private.
- Turn off "Suggest your account to others."
- Control who can comment, message, or duet.
- Avoid linking your phone number or email publicly.

These changes don't make you invisible—but they reduce your digital surface area.

Think Before You Post

Ask yourself three simple questions before posting anything:

1. Who really needs to see this?
2. Could this be used against me or someone I love?
3. Would I be okay with this existing forever?

Because online content is rarely "deleted." Screenshots, data scraping, archive tools—once it's out, it's out.

Some examples of oversharing gone wrong:

- A mother shares a video of her toddler dancing—and it ends up on a fetish site.

- A teenager posts about skipping school—his teacher sees it, and he gets suspended.
- An executive jokes about layoffs—the post goes viral, damaging the company's brand.

Social media is permanent memory without your consent. Use it wisely.

Behind the Scenes: What Your Profile Reveals

Let's run a quick experiment.

Open your main social media profile from a friend's account or in incognito mode. Now look at it as if you're a stranger:

- What personal details can you learn?
- Can someone guess where you live, where you work, or who you're close to?
- Do your photos show patterns, like places you frequent?

Now imagine you're a scammer, recruiter, or stalker.

Still feel comfortable?

Beyond Settings: Social Hygiene

Good privacy isn't just about buttons and toggles—it's about behavior.

- Avoid tagging your exact location in real time.
- Delay vacation photos until after you return.
- Be selective about friend/follow requests—verify profiles.

- Don't post children's full names, birthdays, or school info.
- Use pseudonyms or initials on certain platforms.

And remember: you don't owe anyone an explanation for protecting yourself.

Pro Tips

- Use a "burner" email for social platforms—not your main one.
- Create private friend lists and use them for targeted posts.
- Review your tagged photos regularly—remove yourself if needed.
- Don't accept friend requests from people you don't know—even if they have 50 mutuals.
- Report impersonators immediately.

Healthy Skepticism Is a Strength

Some fear that caring about privacy makes you paranoid or antisocial.

That's nonsense.

Being cautious online doesn't mean you're fearful—it means you're aware. You can still share joy, milestones, and memories. You just do it on your terms, with your eyes open.

Final Thought

Social media gave us the power to broadcast our lives. But with that power comes risk.

The platforms aren't neutral. They reward visibility. They encourage emotional posts, controversial takes, constant engagement.

But your safety comes first.

In the next chapter, we'll shift from platforms to the devices themselves—how your phone, your apps, and your smart home may be quietly listening in.

And how to shut that door.

Checklist: Social Media Privacy Check-Up

- Review and adjust privacy settings on all platforms
- Use strong, unique passwords for each account
- Enable two-factor authentication
- Delete or deactivate old accounts you no longer use
- Regularly audit friends/followers and remove unknowns
- Turn off real-time location sharing
- Pause before you post—think of future consequences

Chapter 5

Smartphones, Apps, and Smart Homes

The Devices That Spy on You

The Spy in Your Pocket

It sits on your nightstand while you sleep. It rides with you in your car, listens while you talk, tracks your steps, and captures your face to unlock itself. It knows where you've been, who you've called, what you've searched, and even how you breathe.

It's your smartphone—and it may be your biggest privacy risk.

Smartphones have transformed our lives. But they've also become surveillance hubs. Not just from the manufacturer or the network provider, but from every app installed on the device—each with its own appetite for data.

When Apps Take More Than They Need

In 2021, a popular weather app was exposed for selling users' exact GPS coordinates to advertisers and data brokers. It asked for location access to give accurate forecasts—but it kept collecting that data in the background, even when the app wasn't open.

Then came the twist: those GPS coordinates were sold not only to marketers but reportedly to government contractors. With no warrant. No consent. No warning.

That app had been downloaded over 50 million times.

And that's just one example.

Here's what mobile apps often request—and what that means for your privacy:

Permission	What They Can Access
Location	Tracks your movements in real time
Camera	May record or snap photos silently
Microphone	Can listen to ambient sound and conversations
Contacts	Exposes your entire social graph
Files/Photos	Reads stored media, sometimes uploads it
Device Info	Captures your model, network, IMEI, behavior analytics

Most users just tap "Allow" during installation. And once granted, apps rarely remind you they're still watching.

How to Audit Your Smartphone Right Now?

Take back control with a quick audit:

On Android:

- Go to Settings > Privacy > Permission Manager.
- Review each category (Location, Microphone, Camera, etc.).
- Revoke access for apps that don't need it.

On iOS:

- Open Settings > Privacy & Security.
- Tap each permission type and check which apps have access.
- Toggle off unnecessary access.
- Turn on App Tracking Transparency to block cross-app tracking.

Also, delete apps you no longer use. Old apps can still collect data or become security risks.

The Hidden Cost of "Free" Apps

If you're wondering how free apps make money—here's the answer: you.

Free flashlight app? It might be harvesting your location and selling it. A wallpaper app? Possibly logging your app usage habits. Even fitness trackers have been caught sharing sensitive health and movement data with advertisers.

In many cases, these apps:

- Use third-party analytics SDKs (Software Development Kits) that siphon your behavior
- Sell data to brokers who link it with purchases and browsing history
- Track your interactions—even when the app is closed

Your phone becomes a goldmine—and you're not the one cashing in.

The Smart Home: More Convenient, Less Private

Smart speakers. Smart bulbs. Smart locks. Smart TVs. The Internet of Things (IoT) has turned our homes into connected ecosystems—but every device with a microphone, camera, or sensor can become a listening post.

Let's unpack the risks:

Smart Speakers (Alexa, Google Home)

- Always listening for a wake word.
- Sometimes trigger unintentionally and record conversations.
- Audio snippets are often sent to cloud servers—some reviewed by humans.

In 2019, it was revealed that Amazon employees listened to thousands of Alexa recordings, including arguments, intimate moments, and even disturbing events—without users realizing it.

Smart TVs

- Collect viewing history, voice commands, and menu navigation patterns.
- Some models have been caught tracking which USB movies you play, even if they're offline.

One major brand was fined in the U.S. for tracking users without clear consent and selling viewing data to advertisers.

Baby Monitors & Security Cameras

- Vulnerable to hacks if default passwords aren't changed.
- Cases exist where strangers accessed baby monitors to talk to children.

These aren't science fiction stories. They've been reported in mainstream news—and the culprits were often just opportunistic hackers using free software tools.

Weakest Link: Your Wi-Fi Network

Many smart devices are poorly secured. They lack updates, use default credentials, or transmit data unencrypted. Once breached, they can give attackers a backdoor into your home network.

Real-world case: A security researcher hacked a smart lightbulb that hadn't been updated. From there, he jumped onto the Wi-Fi network and accessed other devices—including the user's laptop.

It's not the bulb that's dangerous—it's the door it opens.

Expert Insights

Interview Excerpt – Rajiv Deshmukh, IoT Security Analyst, CyberSec India

"People assume smart devices are harmless because they're small or 'non-computing.' But every device with a chip is a potential spy. Many manufacturers cut corners on security to lower cost. Consumers are left exposed—often without realizing it."

He adds: *"Always change default passwords. Segment your smart devices onto a guest network. And don't buy 'smart' just for the sake of it. Ask yourself: Do I really need my coffee maker connected to the internet?"*

Pro Tips for Device Privacy

- Turn off voice assistants if you don't use them regularly
- Place smart speakers away from bedrooms or bathrooms
- Disable "cloud storage" for recordings unless necessary
- Always change default login credentials
- Create a separate Wi-Fi network for IoT devices
- Keep firmware updated (set a calendar reminder every 3 months)
- Cover laptop webcams when not in use
- Don't allow blanket permissions—use "Ask Every Time" where possible

Behind the Scenes: How End-to-End Encryption Works?

You might have heard of "end-to-end encryption" in apps like Signal or WhatsApp.

Here's what it means—simply:

- Only the sender and receiver can read the message.
- Even the service provider (e.g., WhatsApp or Signal) can't see it.
- The message is scrambled (encrypted) before it leaves your device and only unscrambled (decrypted) on the recipient's phone.
- Anyone who intercepts it in transit sees gibberish.

This is why end-to-end encryption is powerful. It prevents governments, ISPs, or rogue actors from snooping—even if they tap into your data stream.

Use encrypted tools whenever possible for communication and file sharing.

Final Thought

Your smartphone and smart home devices are powerful tools. But they're not neutral.

They're shaped by corporate incentives, often built with insufficient privacy protections, and capable of watching far more than you realize.

You don't have to become a hermit. But you do need to become intentional.

Because when every device becomes a potential observer, awareness becomes your strongest defense.

Checklist: Device Privacy Health Check

- Review app permissions on your phone
- Delete apps you no longer use
- Turn off location when not needed
- Update firmware on smart home devices
- Create a separate guest network for IoT
- Use encrypted messaging for private conversations
- Cover webcams and mute mics when not in use

Part II

Privacy in the Workplace

Protecting Your Data in Your Professional Life

Your Boss Might Be Watching. Your Clients Definitely Are.

When we think about digital privacy, most of us imagine our homes, our phones, or our social media profiles. But one of the most overlooked—and increasingly monitored—spaces is the one we spend most of our waking hours in: the workplace.

Whether you're logging into a company computer at a corporate office, replying to emails from your home desk, or juggling freelance gigs on your personal laptop, your professional life is tethered to data. And every digital move you make at work leaves a trail.

But here's the tricky part: you don't own the tools you're working on—and in many cases, you don't control what's being monitored.

Employers track internet use, read internal messages, capture keystrokes, analyze productivity dashboards, and even use AI to assess tone in customer calls. And increasingly, these practices extend to remote workers, gig economy platforms, and even independent contractors. Some companies go as far as taking screenshots every 10 minutes or monitoring whether your webcam detects your face during work hours.

Freelancers aren't immune either. You might be the one collecting client data—names, addresses, payment details—but how you store and secure it matters. One wrong move, one unsecured spreadsheet, and you're not just risking embarrassment—you could be breaching laws, losing trust, and damaging your reputation.

The lines between personal and professional devices have blurred. Bring Your Own Device (BYOD) policies mean your private phone might carry company apps. Remote work means your home network might now host sensitive data. Your workplace habits—and the policies behind them—now reach into your living room, your inbox, and your cloud backups.

Why This Part Matters?

You may not be able to opt out of using work tools. But you can:

- Learn how employer monitoring works—and where the limits lie
- Understand your rights (and responsibilities) depending on where you live and work
- Develop strategies to protect personal data at work
- Set up safeguards to avoid accidentally mishandling client or company information
- Become a privacy champion in your workplace, influencing safer digital habits company-wide

Whether you're an employee, a founder, a freelancer, or a manager, your work life is surrounded by digital exposure points.

And this part of the book is here to make sure you're not walking through that minefield blind.

Coming Up Next

We begin with a reality check: just how much does your employer really see?

Let's get to work.

Chapter 6

The Office Knows Everything

Workplace Privacy 101

Welcome to the Monitored Office

Sonia always thought her Slack chats were private. After all, she was messaging a colleague—not a client, not her manager. They were venting about a long meeting, joking about the CEO's obsession with buzzwords. It felt harmless.

Then one morning, her manager pulled her aside.

"We've been reviewing internal communications," he said. "Let's talk about your attitude in team channels."

She froze. Internal communications? She hadn't known her employer had full access to her message history—including private channels.

But they did. And they had the logs to prove it.

Surveillance by Design

In the modern workplace, surveillance isn't always malicious—but it's often invisible.

Employers now have tools to monitor:

Monitoring Method	What It Tracks
Keystroke Logging	Number of keystrokes typed, idle time
Screen Captures	Periodic snapshots of your desktop
Web Activity Logs	Sites visited, time spent on each site
Email Monitoring	Content of messages, attachments, recipients
Chat Archives	Slack, Teams, and other internal messages

Monitoring Method	What It Tracks
Location Tracking	GPS from company phones or fleet vehicles
Badge Systems	Physical movement in office spaces
Time-Tracking Software	Log-ins, log-outs, productivity analytics

Most of this happens in the name of productivity, compliance, or security. But the scope of monitoring can cross into personal territory—especially in hybrid and remote work environments.

Remote Work: Your Home Is Not Off-Limits

Rahul, a remote marketing executive in Bangalore, was using his company-issued laptop at home. One day, he received a feedback report from HR. It included the number of hours he'd stayed "active," times he appeared away from his keyboard, and screenshots showing what he was viewing.

He was shocked. He hadn't been slacking—he just didn't know his webcam-activity monitor was flagging him as "inactive" during long video edits.

That's thc ncw normal.

Popular remote-monitoring tools like Time Doctor, Hubstaff, and Teramind track everything from mouse movement to webcam presence. Some even send alerts to managers if workers don't meet activity thresholds.

The line between oversight and overreach is blurry.

Are They Allowed to Do This?

It depends on where you work.

United States

In the U.S., employers have wide latitude to monitor employees—especially on company-owned devices and networks. Federal law permits monitoring emails, internet use, and even phone calls, provided there's a "legitimate business reason."

In most states, companies don't have to notify employees about monitoring, although it's often disclosed in employment contracts or IT policies.

European Union

In contrast, EU employees enjoy far stronger protections under the General Data Protection Regulation (GDPR).

Key principles:

- Monitoring must be proportionate and justified
- Employees must be informed in advance
- Personal data must be minimized and securely handled
- Workers have the right to access data collected about them

In France and Germany, excessive employee surveillance has been legally challenged and fined. In 2021, a Spanish supermarket chain was fined €2.5 million for secretly using facial recognition on employees without consent.

Know What You Signed

When you joined your company, you likely signed an employment agreement or IT policy. Buried in that fine print may be a clause that says:

> *"All activity conducted on company devices or networks may be monitored and recorded."*

That includes:

- Personal emails sent via company Wi-Fi
- Messages on "private" Slack channels
- File transfers via USB
- Sites visited during lunch breaks

The law often distinguishes between expectation of privacy and ownership of tools. If you're using their laptop, their network, and their software—you may have little legal ground to object.

Story: Tracked by the Company Car

Nina was a regional sales lead in Pune. Her company issued her a phone and a vehicle with built-in GPS. She didn't mind—it made expense reporting easier.

One Friday, she left early to pick up her son from school and skipped a client visit. The following Monday, her manager asked about it.

They'd reviewed the vehicle's GPS logs. They knew where she went. The conversation ended with a warning.

She wasn't reprimanded for poor work—but for leaving a digital trail.

Your Rights (and Wrongs)

Depending on your region, you may be entitled to:

- A copy of your HR file
- A list of devices and tools being monitored
- Notification before surveillance begins
- The right to refuse access to personal devices

But few employees ever ask. Why?

- Fear of appearing suspicious
- Lack of awareness
- Company culture that discourages pushback

Knowing your rights isn't rebellion—it's responsibility. Privacy at work starts with understanding where your boundaries lie.

Expert Interview

Excerpt – Alisha Mendiratta, Labor Law Attorney, Mumbai

> *"Most employees don't realize that even casual platforms like Slack, Zoom, and Google Chat are often archived. In India, the legal framework is evolving, but in practice, the power imbalance favors employers. Employees must assume that company devices and accounts are monitored—and adjust behavior accordingly."*

She adds:

> *"Use personal devices for personal matters. Avoid logging into private emails from work networks. And ask HR to clarify the company's surveillance policy—you're entitled to that transparency."*

Pro Tips: Stay Smart at Work

- Treat work devices as public tools, not personal ones
- Don't use office email for personal accounts (e.g. shopping, banking)
- Assume internal messages are not private, even in "DMs"
- Log out of personal accounts before handing in company equipment
- Use your own device and internet for sensitive communications
- Ask HR for a written copy of your digital monitoring policy
- Never store personal files (photos, tax returns, medical records) on work laptops

Final Thought

Privacy at work isn't just about surveillance—it's about trust. Your employer trusts you to do your job. You trust them not to cross a line.

But trust without transparency can breed resentment, fear, or accidental exposure.

By knowing what tools are watching, understanding your rights, and setting boundaries between work and personal life, you don't just protect yourself—you create a healthier work culture for everyone.

In the next chapter, we'll tackle the blurring of those boundaries even further—with Bring Your Own Device (BYOD) policies and the challenges of remote work environments.

Checklist: Work Privacy Best Practices

- Don't use work email for personal sign-ups
- Review your IT policy for monitoring clauses
- Use a separate browser profile for work
- Avoid storing personal files on company systems
- Ask HR if internal messages and chats are archived
- Assume company tools are company property—including the data inside them

Chapter 7

Bring Your Own Device (BYOD) & Remote Work

Blurring Home and Work

The New Workplace Has No Walls

Arjun sat on his couch, coffee in hand, laptop on his knees. His toddler watched cartoons nearby while he responded to a Slack ping from a client. It was 10:30 a.m., and his personal MacBook was also his work laptop. One device. Two worlds.

That same night, he got a calendar invite from HR—subject line: Performance Monitoring Review.

Unbeknownst to Arjun, the company's IT department had silently pushed a remote activity-tracking tool onto his system. His personal files weren't touched. But the line felt crossed.

That's the reality of BYOD (Bring Your Own Device) and remote work—a productivity revolution that's turned privacy into a tightrope walk.

One Device, Two Lives

Many companies now let—or even expect—employees to use personal laptops, phones, and tablets for work. It's convenient, cost-effective, and familiar. But it also raises hard questions:

- What happens if a personal device gets hacked while containing client data?
- Can an employer legally access parts of your device to monitor work tools?
- If a device is lost, can IT remotely wipe the whole phone—including private photos or documents?
- What if your child downloads malware onto the same laptop you use for confidential spreadsheets?

BYOD policies blur ownership, control, and privacy. And when something goes wrong, accountability gets messy.

Securing a Shared Device

If you must use one device for both work and personal tasks, here's how to reduce risk:

1. Enable Full-Device Encryption

- Use BitLocker (Windows) or FileVault (Mac)
- Set a strong, unique password—not your fingerprint or face alone
- Encrypt phone storage (Android/iPhone have this by default if locked properly)

Encryption protects your data even if the device is stolen or lost.

2. Create Separate User Profiles

- Windows and macOS both allow multiple users or workspaces
- Keep work files and apps under a separate login or user profile
- This prevents accidental leaks (like sharing a client document during a personal video call)

3. Use Containers or Work Profiles (Mobile)

- Android offers "Work Profiles" that separate apps and data
- Some MDM (Mobile Device Management) solutions create encrypted "containers"
- This allows IT to manage only the work portion of your phone—leaving personal messages untouched

Ask your IT team if this is available before giving blanket permissions.

What If You Lose the Device?

Losing a device is bad. Losing access-controlled, confidential data along with it is worse.

Here's how to prepare:

- Enable remote-wipe functionality (via iCloud, Android Device Manager, or MDM tools)
- Store work documents in encrypted cloud folders—not local drives
- Keep sensitive files behind an additional password or PIN
- Log out of all remote-access platforms (e.g., Slack, Gmail, CRM tools)
- Report to your employer immediately to trigger incident response

Prevention isn't just smart—it may be legally necessary in regulated industries.

The Remote Work Privacy Puzzle

Remote work gives flexibility—but also opens a Pandora's box of privacy issues:

- Monitoring software may track mouse movement, active windows, and keyboard input
- Always-on webcams during team meetings erode personal space
- Location data may be collected by mobile apps used for remote check-ins
- Home networks may not be secure enough for transmitting sensitive client information

In short, working from home doesn't mean you're out of view—it means surveillance follows you there.

Managing Virtual Boundaries

Here are strategies to maintain boundaries while working remotely:

1. Use a Dedicated Work Laptop (If Possible)

This is the cleanest option. If your company provides a device, don't use it for personal browsing, banking, or private messages. Treat it as a monitored tool.

2. Blur Your Background in Meetings

Video conferencing platforms like Zoom, Google Meet, and Microsoft Teams now offer built-in privacy settings:

- Blur backgrounds
- Use a virtual image (professional and distraction-free)
- Turn off video when not needed
- Mute microphone when not speaking

Remember: what's visible (family photos, documents, children) could end up in screen recordings.

Upgrade Your Home Network

- Use strong WPA2 or WPA3 encryption
- Change the default router login and password
- Create a guest network for smart home devices
- Regularly update firmware

This minimizes exposure—especially when confidential files flow through your Wi-Fi.

Real Case: The Freelancer's Overshare

Nidhi, a freelance designer, often worked on client presentations late at night. She used a shared family laptop. One day, her younger brother accidentally uploaded a school project onto a cloud folder she used for a high-profile pharma client.

The client saw it. They weren't amused.

Nidhi lost the contract—not for malice, but for poor data hygiene.

Lesson: even if you're your own boss, you're still responsible for securing client data.

Ask Before You Sync

Before connecting your personal device to any work system, ask:

- Will the company install any monitoring software?
- Can they access my entire device or only specific apps?
- If needed, can they wipe just the work portion remotely?
- What logs are kept, and for how long?
- What happens to my personal data if I leave the company?

If you don't get clear answers, reconsider what you're agreeing to.

Expert Perspective

Interview Excerpt – Kartik Narula, CTO at a remote-first SaaS company

> *"We use a split system—employees access a cloud-based virtual desktop hosted on our secure servers. That way, their personal device isn't at risk, and our data stays within our environment. BYOD doesn't mean zero control. It means smarter architecture."*

He adds:

> *"When companies push intrusive monitoring, they create distrust. Privacy-respecting setups lead to better performance—not worse."*

Pro Tips: BYOD & Remote Privacy Survival

- Use full-disk encryption and secure lock screens
- Don't share your device with family during work hours
- Avoid saving passwords in browsers used for both personal and work access
- Backup critical work files in encrypted cloud storage
- Regularly review what apps have access to what data
- Prefer privacy-centric video conferencing tools when possible
- Know how to perform a remote wipe—test it before you need it

Final Thought

Work is no longer confined to cubicles or desktops. It travels with us—into cafés, bedrooms, airports, and living rooms. But with that freedom comes responsibility.

BYOD and remote work models demand a new level of digital maturity. You must become the boundary-setter. The gatekeeper. The IT admin of your own life.

Because when one device carries both your career and your private world, you can't afford to let either fall into the wrong hands.

Next up, we'll go deeper into your role as a professional custodian of others' data—and what ethical handling really means.

Checklist: BYOD & Remote Work Privacy Protocol

- Use a work-only profile or separate device
- Encrypt everything—files, storage, backups
- Set up remote wipe and test it
- Blur or hide your background in video calls
- Avoid storing client data locally
- Discuss monitoring expectations before signing BYOD agreements
- Upgrade your home network security

Chapter 8

Handling Sensitive Data at Work

Ethics and Best Practices

With Great Data Comes Great Responsibility

Jaya worked in the HR department of a mid-sized firm in Hyderabad. She was efficient, trusted, and meticulous. One evening, while working late from home, she copied a batch of employee salary records onto a USB stick to finish some tasks offline.

The next morning, she couldn't find the drive.

It was never recovered.

The USB contained unencrypted data: names, Aadhaar numbers, salaries, PAN details. Within two weeks, a phishing scam targeted several employees, mimicking the company's payroll vendor.

No firewall could've stopped it. The damage was internal.

This chapter isn't about how data is stolen—it's about how good people mishandle it without meaning to.

Not Just IT's Job

Whether you're in HR, sales, marketing, finance, healthcare, or customer service—if you deal with people's personal information, you're part of the privacy ecosystem.

- An HR officer storing employee records
- A marketing analyst reviewing behavior analytics
- A clinic receptionist booking patient appointments
- A lawyer handling client case files
- A freelancer managing e-commerce orders

In every case, privacy isn't just policy—it's your responsibility.

Data Minimization: Take Only What You Need

One of the core principles of privacy is data minimization: collect only what you truly need, and nothing more.

Ask yourself:

- Do I really need someone's full date of birth—or just their age range?
- Is collecting gender, religion, or marital status necessary for this process?
- Why are we saving old customer contact details from three years ago?

Collecting more data may seem harmless. But every unnecessary data point increases risk:

- If breached, it exposes more than needed
- It creates ethical liability—what if it's misused internally?
- It may violate laws depending on the region

Good practice: Build forms and workflows that default to *minimum necessary information*.

Secure Storage: Locks, Layers, and Encryption

Privacy isn't just about what you collect—it's about how you protect it.

Storage Practice	Risk	Better Practice
Saving files on desktops	Easy to access	Use encrypted folders or drives
Using shared team folders	Accidental exposure	Set role-based permissions
Emailing spreadsheets	Interception risk	Use encrypted cloud links with expiry
Writing passwords on sticky notes	Obvious	Use a password manager

Even well-meaning professionals create vulnerabilities. Make security frictionless:

- Use tools like Google Workspace or Microsoft 365 with proper admin controls
- Enable two-factor authentication on all cloud systems
- Store sensitive data in tools that offer audit trails and access logs
- Avoid saving anything on portable media unless encrypted (and never without password protection)

Proper Disposal: Don't Let Data Linger

How you delete data matters.

Deleting a file from your desktop doesn't remove it permanently. It often sits in a recycle bin—or worse, in backup systems indefinitely.

If you handle sensitive data:

- Understand your company's data retention policy
- Set auto-deletion timers on cloud folders (e.g., 30 days for temp files)
- Shred physical documents containing personal data
- Use tools that support secure erasure for digital files

A real estate firm in the UK was fined under GDPR after it was discovered that outdated customer files—containing bank details—were still accessible on an old system. The breach didn't come from hackers. It came from neglect.

Data Breach Isn't Just a Tech Problem

In 2022, a healthcare worker in Los Angeles was fired—and later charged—after accessing celebrity patient records out of curiosity. They didn't leak it or use it. They just looked.

But in the privacy world, intent doesn't matter. Impact does.

Access without necessity is considered a violation in many jurisdictions.

This is why many hospitals implement role-based access—so front-desk staff can't see medical histories, and surgeons can't see billing data unless required.

If you're in any role handling private data, stick to the boundaries of purpose.

What the Law Says (Plain English Version)

Let's break down some common data protection regulations:

GDPR (Europe)

- Applies to EU residents
- Gives people the right to know what's collected, correct it, delete it
- Organizations must get clear consent for data use
- Huge fines for non-compliance (€20M or 4% of global turnover)

HIPAA (USA, Healthcare)

- Applies to patient data
- Covers storage, access, and disclosure rules
- Violations can lead to both civil and criminal penalties

DPDP Act (India)

- Requires "data fiduciaries" (companies) to protect personal data

- Mandates purpose limitation, consent, and right to erase data
- Non-compliance may lead to large financial penalties

Even if you're not a lawyer, the core idea is simple:

> *Use only what's needed, protect it well, and dispose of it responsibly.*

Story: The Small Business That Paid Big

A boutique travel agency in Singapore ran a campaign for honeymooners. They collected passport numbers, travel dates, and hotel bookings through a Google Form.

Then they got hacked.

The form didn't have proper access controls. Anyone with the link could view submissions. The exposure included passport scans, personal emails, and travel itineraries.

The business didn't survive the public fallout.

Lesson: even small teams handling sensitive data must think like professionals.

Expert Insight

Interview Excerpt – Meera Aiyer, Chief Privacy Officer, FinServe Global

"The biggest misconception is that privacy is a technical issue. In reality, most breaches happen due to human behavior—copying files to the wrong folder, forgetting to revoke access, or failing to delete old data."

She adds:

"We train every employee, not just the IT team. Because data security is like hygiene—it only works when everyone does their part."

Pro Tips: Be a Privacy Champion at Work

- Don't store sensitive files on local drives—use secure cloud storage
- Double-check email recipients before sending confidential info
- Never use personal email for client data
- Use tools that log access (so misuse can be traced)
- Flag risky practices to your manager or IT—speak up early
- Sanitize devices before discarding or recycling
- Delete data when it's no longer needed
- Respect data like it was your own

Final Thought

Every byte of personal data you touch—whether it's a customer's phone number, an employee's ID card, or a patient's medical record—represents real people, real trust, and real consequences.

Privacy at work isn't just compliance. It's character.

You may never see a courtroom or headline. But the way you handle someone else's data reflects the kind of professional—and human—you are.

As we wrap up Part II, remember: privacy isn't someone else's job. It's yours too.

Next, we step out into the world—because privacy isn't just at home or work. It's also at airports, cafés, train stations, and street corners. And it deserves protection there too.

Checklist: Professional Privacy Ethics

- Collect only essential data—avoid overreach
- Encrypt files before storage or transmission
- Restrict access to sensitive data
- Never move unencrypted data via USB or email
- Regularly delete outdated personal records
- Know which laws apply to your industry
- Log incidents—even small ones—for accountability
- Always act as if someone trusted you with their secrets—because they did

Part III

Public Spaces, Society, and the Bigger Picture

Staying Private in a Connected World

You're Being Watched—and Not Just Online

You leave home. Your phone connects to a public Wi-Fi at the airport. CCTV cameras track your path through the terminal. A rideshare app logs your pickup location, your destination, and how long the trip took. Meanwhile, your smart watch silently sends step counts and heart rate data to a server you've never heard of.

You haven't posted anything. You haven't clicked anything. But you've already shared dozens of data points—passively, silently, and most of all, constantly.

This part of the book is about that world—the world beyond your devices and beyond your home. It's the surveillance cameras, data brokers, border checkpoints, law enforcement requests, retail loyalty programs, facial recognition gates, and algorithmic decision-making systems that follow you through society.

And it's about how you can navigate it all with awareness, confidence, and smart resistance.

From Individual Action to Collective Exposure

So far, you've learned how to secure your personal life and workplace. But your privacy doesn't stop at your doorstep or your inbox.

You might use a VPN, tweak your app settings, and encrypt your chats—but still be caught in a surveillance net built by cities, governments, corporations, or even other citizens (think doorbell cams and dashcams).

Your presence in public—physical or digital—generates a shadow. Your location, facial features, movement patterns, purchases, travel history, and even political leanings can be harvested, inferred, and stored without your consent.

And yet, few people know it's happening. Even fewer push back.

Why This Part Matters?

This final section is your next level of privacy awareness. It shows you:

- How your data gets exposed in public spaces like airports, cafés, and city streets
- Why government surveillance is a growing concern in democracies and authoritarian regimes alike
- How location data and travel patterns are bought and sold—sometimes even used in court or against journalists
- What rights you do (or don't) have when it comes to your digital identity in the real world
- How to use privacy tools, smart behaviors, and digital hygiene to reduce exposure without living in fear

It also expands the conversation beyond the individual. Because digital privacy isn't just personal—it's political, economic, and social. It affects how we're governed, how justice is served, and how power operates in the 21st century.

What's Ahead

In the coming chapters, you'll learn how to:

- Avoid risky public Wi-Fi traps and location-based profiling
- Use travel strategies to protect your devices and digital rights
- Understand how governments use your data—and how to push for stronger safeguards
- Build a modern "privacy toolkit" with easy-to-use tools (VPNs, secure browsers, encrypted email, and more)
- Develop habits that protect you and the people around you—even in places where privacy feels optional

We'll also spotlight cases where public data exposure led to wrongful arrests, discrimination, surveillance creep, and institutional overreach—because these stories are becoming more common, and they affect real people.

Privacy Is a Public Matter

Privacy doesn't stop at your phone. It moves with you. And it intersects with how cities are run, how societies function, and how technology is shaping democracy.

By the time you finish this section, you'll understand the wider battlefield—and know how to move through it with your eyes open and your defenses up.

Let's begin with *Chapter 9: On the Move – Travel, Public Wi-Fi, and Location Privacy.*

Because your privacy deserves protection wherever life takes you.

Chapter 9

On the Move

Travel, Public Wi-Fi, and Location Privacy

You Don't Have to Log in to Be Watched

Deepika landed at Frankfurt Airport, connected to the free Wi-Fi, and opened her banking app. She just wanted to check her balance before heading to her hotel. It took 45 seconds.

Three days later, her account was flagged for suspicious login attempts—from an IP in Ukraine.

She hadn't been hacked. She'd been watched. A man-in-the-middle attacker had intercepted her unencrypted traffic on the public network. It happens every day.

The world beyond your home is full of conveniences—free Wi-Fi, location-based apps, seamless airport experiences. But it's also packed with invisible data traps.

Let's unpack how to protect your privacy when you're in motion.

Public Wi-Fi: Free Isn't Safe

Public Wi-Fi is everywhere—airports, cafés, hotels, libraries, malls. But that convenience comes with risk:

What Can Go Wrong?

Risk	Description
Snooping	Anyone on the same network can intercept your unencrypted data

Risk	Description
Fake Hotspots	A rogue network mimics the real one to steal info ("Evil Twin")
Session Hijacking	Attackers grab your active login session (like Gmail or Facebook)
Credential Theft	Login forms and passwords can be logged if unprotected

What You Should Never Do on Public Wi-Fi?

- Don't log into bank accounts or financial services
- Avoid entering sensitive personal info
- Don't access work portals unless using a secure connection
- Don't assume HTTPS protects everything (some apps still transmit unencrypted data)

Safe Browsing on the Go

If you must use public Wi-Fi:

- Use a VPN: Encrypts all traffic between your device and the internet
- Use Your Phone's Hotspot: Cellular data is usually safer than open Wi-Fi
- Turn Off Auto-Connect: Prevents your phone from joining risky networks unknowingly
- Forget the Network After Use: Prevents background reconnections

- Use Encrypted DNS: Tools like DNS over HTTPS (DoH) help avoid DNS leaks

Remember: public Wi-Fi is a convenience, not a safe zone. Treat it like a public toilet—use it when you have to, but don't linger, and always wash up after.

Location Tracking: Always On, Always Sending

Your phone knows where you are—even when you think it doesn't.

Apps regularly collect GPS coordinates, nearby Wi-Fi networks, Bluetooth beacons, and cell tower signals to pinpoint your location. Often, they do it in the background.

Studies show that many apps access location data thousands of times per day, even when not in active use.

Why It Matters?

- Advertisers build location-based profiles to target ads
- Data brokers buy and sell movement data (including visits to clinics, religious centers, etc.)
- Law enforcement sometimes purchases location data without warrants
- Stalkers have used leaked app permissions to find victims

How to Regain Control of Your Location?

Audit App Permissions

Go to Settings > Privacy > Location Services

- Review which apps have "Always," "While Using," or "Never" access
- Remove location access for apps that don't need it (e.g., calculators, games, shopping apps)

Disable Location History

- Google, Apple, and others store long-term logs of your movements
- Visit your account dashboard and pause or delete location history

Use "Approximate" Location

Modern devices allow approximate location for apps that don't need precision. Turn it on.

Turn Off Wi-Fi and Bluetooth When Not in Use

These signals are often used to track your proximity to beacons in malls, airports, and city streets.

Travel Privacy: Crossing Borders, Carrying Data

When you travel, you carry more than luggage. Your phone, laptop, tablet, and even e-reader contain massive amounts of personal and professional data.

But at borders, your privacy rights may change drastically.

Can Customs Search Your Devices?

- In countries like the U.S., Canada, and Australia, border agents can inspect devices without a warrant
- Refusing may lead to denial of entry, device confiscation, or extended questioning
- Some jurisdictions can copy data, store it temporarily, or ask for passwords
- Even encrypted files may raise suspicion if not explained

Travel Privacy Best Practices

Risk	Travel-Proof Solution
Device seizure	✅ Carry a minimal travel device with only essential data
Cloud data exposure	✅ Log out of cloud apps and use encrypted vaults
Data theft during transit	✅ Use full-device encryption (BitLocker, FileVault, etc.)

Risk	Travel-Proof Solution
Suspicion from encryption	✅ Create decoy user profiles with minimal content
Loss/theft	✅ Enable remote wipe and device tracking tools

Also, back up everything before you leave home. If you lose a device or wipe it under duress, your data is still safe.

Cameras, Sensors, and City Surveillance

It's not just your devices tracking you—cities themselves are watching.

Across the globe:

- CCTV cameras track movement in streets, malls, buses, and train stations
- License plate readers (LPRs) record where and when your car was seen
- Facial recognition systems scan for matches against criminal or protest databases
- Public Wi-Fi beacons track device MAC addresses for "foot traffic analysis"

Surveillance is sold as safety, but it's often implemented without oversight or consent.

In Delhi, over 1.4 lakh (140,000+) CCTV cameras record citizens daily. No independent data protection body exists to regulate them. In London, citizens appear on camera more than 300 times a day.

You Can't Hide—But You Can Harden

- You can't avoid every camera. But you can take steps to reduce your exposure:
- Use a privacy screen on your laptop or phone in public
- Turn off Wi-Fi and Bluetooth unless actively using them
- Don't log into sensitive accounts on airport/hotel devices
- Dress neutrally and avoid wearing identifiable accessories (e.g., protest pins) in high-surveillance areas
- Be aware of facial recognition deployments—some cities (e.g., San Francisco) have banned them in public use. Know your city's laws.

Pro Tips: Mobility Without Sacrifice

- Use a privacy-first VPN when traveling
- Download offline maps instead of using live GPS
- Disable camera and mic permissions for most apps by default
- Switch to airplane mode when not needing connectivity
- Carry a travel burner phone or laptop for high-risk travel (journalists, activists, professionals with sensitive files)

Final Thought

Every time you walk through a public square, connect to an airport network, or use your phone in a new city, you leave behind digital footprints.

These footprints can be used to help, harm, or sell to you.

Privacy on the move isn't about paranoia—it's about preparation. You have the tools. You just need to use them.

Next, we'll look at the role of governments in the data ecosystem—and how the same institutions tasked with protecting your rights are often the ones watching most closely.

Checklist: Travel & Public Privacy Tips

- Never access banking or sensitive data over public Wi-Fi
- Use a VPN when on any non-home network
- Turn off Wi-Fi and Bluetooth in crowded or unknown locations
- Enable device encryption and remote wipe features
- Avoid carrying unnecessary data across borders
- Research local privacy laws before traveling
- Consider using privacy tools (e.g., Tor, ProtonVPN, encrypted messengers)

Chapter 10

The Surveillance Society

Government, Law Enforcement, and You

The Quiet Expansion of the Watchtower

At 2:13 a.m., a knock shattered the silence outside Ravi's apartment in Bengaluru. The police had come looking for his cousin. They didn't have a warrant in hand—but they knew Ravi's IP address, GPS location from a ride-hailing app, and had transcripts of WhatsApp chats from his cousin's cloud backup.

He hadn't done anything wrong.

But Ravi was now in a digital dragnet—watched, profiled, and detained—not because of what he did, but because of who he was connected to.

That's the reality of modern surveillance.

Governments today play a strange double role: they're privacy's protectors on paper, and its largest violators in practice.

When the State Sees All: From PRISM to Predictive Policing

In 2013, Edward Snowden—then a contractor for the U.S. National Security Agency (NSA)—leaked documents revealing a vast, global surveillance program: PRISM.

What PRISM did was simple, chilling, and legal under U.S. law at the time: it siphoned user data from tech giants like Google, Apple, Microsoft, and Facebook—without needing individual warrants. Emails, chats, file uploads, video calls, even search histories were quietly collected.

You didn't have to be a terrorist. You just had to be interesting—or connected to someone who was.

Today, PRISM has been largely replaced by more advanced and often covert surveillance systems. But the mindset remains. Around the world:

- Facial recognition systems scan crowds in real time
- Predictive policing algorithms identify who's "likely" to commit a crime
- Mass metadata collection flags patterns, associates, locations
- Automatic license plate readers track vehicle movement in cities and highways
- Social media monitoring software watches protests, dissent, and activism

These tools are often deployed with no public debate, no opt-out, and little oversight.

When Law Enforcement Wants Your Data

You don't need to be under investigation to be part of a data request.

Police and intelligence agencies routinely request:

Type of Data	Who Has It	Can Be Accessed?
Call records	Telcos	✅ Without content, often without a warrant
GPS/location	Telecoms, apps	❗ Increasingly requires warrant in some countries

Type of Data	Who Has It	Can Be Accessed?
Emails, chats	Tech companies (e.g., Google, Meta)	✅ Via subpoena or court order
Photos/videos	Cloud services (Google Photos, iCloud)	✅ Often shared unless encrypted
Browsing history	ISPs, some apps	✅ Subject to national laws
Biometric data	Government programs (Aadhaar, DMV, etc.)	✅ Available under court request or policy

Real Example: The U.S. Supreme Court Ruling (Carpenter v. United States, 2018)

In this landmark case, the Court ruled that law enforcement needs a warrant to access historical cellphone location data. Chief Justice John Roberts wrote:

> "A person does not surrender all Fourth Amendment protection by venturing into the public sphere."

It was a turning point—but applies only to the U.S., and only to specific kinds of data.

Elsewhere? It's often still open season on your digital trail.

CCTV, Smart Cities, and the Normalization of Being Watched

Surveillance used to be physical: a man in a trench coat, following you discreetly. Now? It's algorithmic, omnipresent, and normalized.

CCTV Statistics by Region (as of 2025):

Country	Est. Cameras	Notes
China	>500 million	Often combined with facial recognition
UK	~6 million	Highest per capita in Europe
India	~300,000 in Delhi alone	Deployed without citizen consent
USA	~50 million	Used by law enforcement and private businesses
UAE	~250,000 in Dubai	Integrated with AI policing systems

Cities pitch cameras as safety tools. But without oversight, they become tools of control.

Case: The Detroit Facial Recognition Scandal

In 2020, a Black man named Robert Williams was wrongfully arrested after facial recognition software matched his photo to surveillance footage. He had nothing to do with the crime. The tech was wrong—but the jail time was real.

What Are Your Rights? (And Do They Matter?)

Privacy laws vary widely:

Country/Region	Core Protections	Surveillance Loopholes
EU (GDPR)	Explicit consent, data minimization, right to access/delete	Some exemptions for national security
India	Draft DPDP Act (2023–25) gives individual rights	No independent data protection authority as of 2025
USA	Fourth Amendment protection; sectoral privacy laws	FISA, PATRIOT Act allow mass surveillance for "security"
Canada/Australia	Stronger workplace and medical privacy	Weak safeguards for metadata and location tracking

Key Legal Trends:

- Warrants now required for GPS phone tracking (U.S., EU)
- Encryption is legal—but may attract scrutiny in authoritarian countries

- Social media posts are often considered "public domain" by courts
- Biometric data is increasingly regulated—but patchy enforcement

The Chilling Effect: When Awareness Becomes Self-Censorship

Knowing you're watched changes how you behave.

This phenomenon, called the " chilling effect" , leads to:

- People avoiding protests
- Journalists watering down stories
- Citizens refraining from searching politically sensitive topics
- Employees self-censoring messages on workplace platforms

It's not just surveillance. It's psychological control.

The Line Between Safety and Suppression

Governments defend surveillance with one word: security.

But who defines the threat?

- Are whistleblowers "threats"?
- Are protesters "rioters"?
- Are political dissidents "foreign agents"?

Every surveillance state starts by promising safety. But without transparency and checks, it drifts into suppression.

What You Can Do (Yes, You)?

You're not powerless. Here's how to regain agency:

Know the Laws Where You Live

- Look up your local data protection authority
- Learn when law enforcement can request data—and what they need
- Push for transparency reports from tech companies and governments

Use Strong Encryption

- Encrypted messaging (Signal, ProtonMail)
- Secure cloud backups
- Full-device encryption on phones/laptops

Ask Questions

- Ask your city if public cameras use facial recognition
- Ask your school or employer if your devices are being monitored
- Demand public hearings before surveillance expansions

Support Advocacy

- Organizations like EFF, Access Now, Internet Freedom Foundation fight for your rights
- Share their campaigns. Donate. Write to your elected reps.

Final Thought

Governments were supposed to protect your privacy. Instead, many learned to weaponize it.

But awareness is your first shield. Action is your first strike.

Surveillance thrives in silence. But once you see the system, you can demand better.

In the next chapter, we'll move beyond governments—to the even murkier world of data brokers, corporate algorithms, and digital injustice.

Because if the state sees all, corporations sell it all.

Chapter 11

Building Your Privacy Toolkit

Tools and Techniques

From Awareness to Action

Reading about surveillance is one thing. But doing something about it? That's where you take your power back.

In this chapter, we move from the theoretical to the tactical. This is your toolbox—your digital privacy survival kit—with real tools, real strategies, and real protection.

You don't need to be a hacker. You don't need to spend money. You just need to take a few smart steps.

Secure Browsing – Your First Line of Defense

Your browser is often the first place data gets scooped. Every ad, cookie, and embedded script is a potential spy.

Recommended Browsers:

- Brave: Blocks ads and trackers by default. Built-in Tor mode.
- Firefox (with tweaks): Strong open-source browser. Use privacy settings and extensions.
- Tor Browser: For high privacy needs. Hides your IP, encrypts traffic 3 times. Slower, but effective.

Action Steps:

Adjusting Firefox for Privacy:

1. Go to `Settings > Privacy & Security`
2. Select `Strict` under Enhanced Tracking Protection
3. Scroll down and disable `Telemetry` and `Data Collection`
4. Install extensions: uBlock Origin, Privacy Badger, HTTPS Everywhere

VPNs – Shield Your Internet Traffic

A Virtual Private Network (VPN) encrypts your internet traffic and hides your IP address.

But not all VPNs are created equal.

Trusted VPNs (2025):

- ProtonVPN (free plan available, no logs, Swiss-based)
- Mullvad (anonymous signup, accepts cash payments)
- IVPN (strict no-logs, open source clients)

Avoid:

- Free VPNs that log data (Hola, TurboVPN, Opera VPN)
- VPNs with unclear ownership or based in surveillance-heavy jurisdictions

Quick VPN Setup:

1. Download from official website (never app store clones)
2. Select closest server for speed
3. Turn on "Kill Switch" to block internet if VPN drops
4. Enable auto-start on boot

Use a VPN especially on public Wi-Fi, during travel, or when researching sensitive topics.

Encrypted Messaging – No Middleman Reading Your Chats

Every text you send over regular SMS is like a postcard—anyone can read it.

Encrypted messengers wrap your messages in digital armor.

Best Private Messaging Apps:

- Signal: End-to-end encrypted, open source, minimal metadata
- Session: Doesn't require a phone number, runs over onion routing
- Threema: Swiss-based, paid app, no contact syncing

WhatsApp is encrypted, but owned by Meta (Facebook). Metadata and backups may still be accessed.

How to Switch to Signal:

1. Install Signal from signal.org
2. Register your phone number
3. Invite contacts to join (it's free)
4. Enable disappearing messages in chats for sensitive conversations

Password Managers – One Strong Lock for All Doors

You cannot remember 50 strong passwords. And you shouldn't try.

Use a password manager to generate and store unique, unguessable passwords for each service.

Best Password Managers:

- Bitwarden (free, open-source, encrypted)
- 1Password (paid, strong security reputation)
- KeePassXC (local, not cloud-based, best for advanced users)

Getting Started with Bitwarden:

1. Create a master password (long + unique + memorable phrase)
2. Use the browser extension or mobile app
3. Enable 2FA for Bitwarden account
4. Import or save credentials as you go

Multi-Factor Authentication – Your Backup Barrier

Even if someone steals your password, MFA (multi-factor authentication) stops them cold.

It's like needing a key and a fingerprint to open the door.

Best MFA Tools:

- Authenticator apps (e.g., Google Authenticator, Authy, Aegis)
- Hardware keys (e.g., YubiKey, SoloKey)
- Biometrics + PIN (for devices)

Enable 2FA on Key Accounts:

- Gmail: ` Google Account > Security > 2-Step Verification`
- Facebook: ` Settings > Security and Login > Use two-factor`
- PayPal, banking apps, cloud storage, social media—enable 2FA everywhere it's offered

Block the Trackers – You're Not the Product Anymore

Trackers follow your clicks, purchases, and habits.

Block them. Break their business model.

Top Tools:

- uBlock Origin: Powerful content blocker
- Privacy Badger: Learns which third-party requests are tracking you
- DuckDuckGo Privacy Essentials: Easy tracker blocking in browser
- ClearURLs: Removes tracking codes from links

Disable Ad Personalization:

- Google: https://adssettings.google.com → Turn off ad personalization
- Apple: ` Settings > Privacy > Tracking > Allow Apps to Request to Track` → Off
- Facebook: ` Settings > Ads > Ad Settings` → Limit ad use of activity and interests

Email Aliases & Data Removal – Opt Out of the Game

Your real email is a data goldmine.

Tools to Mask or Delete:

- SimpleLogin / AnonAddy: Create aliases like ` newsletter@alias.com` → forwards to real inbox
- Firefox Relay: Free aliases to hide real email
- DeleteMe, Incogni, Optery: Help you remove your data from data broker websites

How to Start with SimpleLogin?

1. Sign up at simplelogin.io
2. Create an alias like ` amazon@alias.simplelogin.com`
3. Forward to your personal email
4. Disable or delete alias anytime—it's disposable

One Day = One Habit

You don't need to fix everything today. But if you act one step at a time, you'll build a fortress.

Day	Privacy Habit
1	Install and set up a password manager
2	Switch to a privacy browser
3	Enable 2FA on email and banking
4	Install Signal and try it with a friend
5	Configure phone to block app tracking
6	Set up VPN on your devices
7	Create 3 email aliases for risky signups

In one week, you've outpaced 90% of internet users in privacy hygiene.

Final Words: You’ve Got This

You’re not powerless. You’re not too late.

The internet wants you to believe that your data is gone and you can't do anything about it. But you can. Right now. With tools that are free, tested, and effective.

Privacy isn’t about paranoia. It’s about autonomy, control, and dignity.

Use these tools. Build your defenses. Teach your family. Share your knowledge.

You’re no longer just a user. You’re your own privacy advocate.

Chapter 12

Staying in Control

Habits for a Privacy-Conscious Life

Privacy Isn't a Destination—It's a Way of Thinking

You've locked down your browser. You've encrypted your messages. You've turned off location tracking and taught your family how to spot scams.

But the truth is, privacy isn't something you "set and forget." It's not just about tools. It's a way of living in a digital world where awareness is power.

This chapter is about making privacy stick—not just as a checklist, but as a lifestyle.

Because the internet keeps changing. Apps update, companies shift policies, laws evolve, and new threats emerge. But the one thing that doesn't change?

Your mindset. Your habits. Your watchfulness.

Build the Muscle: Skepticism Without Cynicism

Every time a popup asks for permission...

Every time an email urges you to click...

Every time a friend shares a viral quiz asking for your birth month, your pet's name, and your favorite city...

Ask yourself one thing:

- What am I giving away?

A privacy-conscious life starts with micro-moments of skepticism:

- Do I need to install this app?
- Is this Wi-Fi connection safe?
- Who really benefits if I click this ad?

Skepticism isn't fear. It's just awareness in motion. Think of it as digital street smarts. You're not shutting yourself off—you're moving smarter.

Stay in the Loop – Privacy Is Evolving

The tools you use today may change tomorrow. That's not failure—it's normal.

To stay sharp, follow people and publications who track privacy developments. Here are a few worth bookmarking:

Trusted Privacy News Sources:

- RestorePrivacy.com – Tool reviews, breach alerts, how-tos
- EFF.org – The Electronic Frontier Foundation's updates on digital rights
- PrivacyGuides.org – Community-driven advice for practical privacy
- Mozilla Blog -https://blog.mozilla.org – Tech insights with a privacy-first angle
- The Markup - https://themarkup.org – Investigative journalism on data and algorithmic accountability

Subscribe to their newsletters. Follow them on privacy-friendly social media like Mastodon. Use RSS if you want to keep it simple.

Help Others Level Up

Privacy isn't something we can fight for alone.

Your elderly parents who click phishing links. Your teenage cousin who overshares on TikTok. Your friend who still uses "123456" as their password.

They need your help.

How to Spread the Knowledge:

- Set up Signal for a friend
- Offer to install a password manager on a parent's phone
- Host a 15-minute "privacy lunch" at your office
- Share this book (yes, this one!) with your network

You become the ripple. Their safety improves because of you. That's how change starts— one conversation, one tool, one "aha" moment at a time.

Vote With Your Wallet (and Voice)

Your privacy choices matter—especially your purchases.

Some companies design products with surveillance baked in. Others fight for your rights

Privacy-Respecting Brands:

- Proton: Offers encrypted email, VPN, calendar
- Mozilla: Builds privacy-first tools like Firefox and Relay
- Purism: Manufactures hardware with privacy as a core feature

- Librem & Fairphone: Ethical smartphones with data control
- DuckDuckGo: A search engine that doesn't track you

When you support these companies, you're sending a clear message:

"Privacy matters. Design for it."

And beyond spending? Speak up.

How to Advocate:

- Email your local representatives about supporting privacy legislation
- Comment publicly on regulatory proposals (e.g., data protection rules)
- Join online campaigns via groups like the EFF or Access Now
- Leave feedback in app stores when tools violate your data trust

You don't need to be loud. You just need to be clear.

Good News: The Tide Is Turning

Here's the most hopeful part of all this:

You're not alone. And you're not fighting a losing battle.

In 2025, we're seeing real momentum:

- Apple and Google are adding more privacy controls (because users demanded it)
- New laws like GDPR, CCPA, and India's DPDP are forcing companies to rethink data hoarding

- Users are leaving platforms that abuse their trust
- Startups are winning customers by making privacy a selling point

Public awareness is rising. And so is resistance.

This is the beginning of a new digital culture—one where you're not just data, you're a human being with rights, preferences, and boundaries.

Your Privacy Pact (A Final Checklist)

Here's your closing habit loop—one you can revisit anytime.

Habit	Frequency
Audit app permissions	Monthly
Update your password manager	Quarterly
Refresh your privacy settings on Google/Facebook	Every 6 months
Back up encrypted files	Monthly
Teach someone a privacy tip	Whenever you can
Read a trusted privacy update	Weekly

You don't need to be perfect. You just need to be consistent.

The Last Word: You Are in Control

Let's be honest—most people give up on privacy because it feels hopeless.

But you didn't.

You read. You learned. You acted. And now, you see the truth:

> *Privacy is not about hiding. It's about choosing what you share—and with whom.*

You're not running. You're not unplugging. You're living smart. You're choosing freedom with intention.

Keep questioning. Keep teaching. Keep adapting.

And never forget: in a world where your data is currency, protecting your privacy is an act of self-respect.

Part IV

Deep Dive for the Privacy-Conscious Future

We've come a long way. By now, you've examined the digital footprints you leave behind, understood the tools and choices that protect or expose your identity, and realized how privacy is affected not just by your actions, but also by the actions of those around you — employers, platforms, governments, and even the devices you trust.

But the landscape is shifting fast. The old threats haven't disappeared — they've simply become more complex, more embedded, more invisible.

And the new threats? They're coming from directions few imagined a decade ago: AI systems that mimic your face and voice, invisible trackers that follow you across devices, therapy apps that claim to heal but record your every vulnerability, and machines that inch ever closer to decoding your emotions and thoughts.

This part of the book is for those who understand that real privacy in the modern world means playing both defense and offense.

It's no longer enough to use a VPN or disable ad tracking. The stakes have changed — and so must the strategies.

Welcome to the deep end of digital privacy.

Here, we don't just react. We investigate, dissect, and anticipate. We go beyond cookie banners and privacy settings to look at systemic patterns — how privacy is shaped by law, eroded by design, exploited by industry, and reclaimed by those who care enough to push back.

We'll explore how new technologies operate in gray areas of legality and ethics, how companies nudge users into surrendering consent they don't understand, and how the very architecture of our digital lives is built around surveillance as a default.

We'll also explore how some are resisting — by designing privacy-first systems, crafting intelligent legislation, and demanding accountability.

And while this section dives deeper into legal frameworks, AI risks, data ecosystems, and technical defenses, it always comes back to one thing: your power to choose.

To pause before downloading. To say no to predatory apps. To support platforms that respect your dignity. To protect not only your data but your values.

Because privacy is no longer a personal preference. It's a human right under siege.

If the first parts of this book were about awareness, this one is about preparedness and action. It's about being the person in your circle who not only knows better — but does better. The one who can explain what a data broker is, how facial recognition threatens civil liberties, or why a seemingly innocent AI chatbot may be storing everything you say.

It's about moving from private to empowered.

So, take a deep breath. This isn't fear-mongering — it's your upgrade. Your deeper layer of armor. Your invitation to not just survive the digital age — but shape it.

Chapter 13

Emerging Privacy Laws & AI Regulation

Why Privacy Law Is Finally Catching Up?

Privacy laws began as afterthoughts. Ten years ago, most regulations focused on consent forms and cookie banners. Now, nations worldwide are passing robust rules that govern data collection, use, deletion, profiling, and notably— AI systems.

Across the globe, we've entered a legal era where:

- Governments mandate explainable AI
- Companies must allow users to opt-out of automated decisions
- Individuals can demand deletion of data that powers AI models

You've seen the headlines: GDPR in Europe. CCPA/CPRA in California. India's DPDP Act on the way. The EU's AI Act. Colorado's AI transparency law. Brazil's LGPD. Japan's APPI updates.

They all serve one mission: protect real people in a world of automated tools.

13.2 Global Snapshot: What's New— and Why It Matters?

European Union – GDPR + AI Act

- GDPR already grants fundamental rights: access, deletion (right to erasure), portability, informed consent
- The AI Act adds:

- Risk-based classification of systems (from low to "unacceptable" risk)
- Bans on AI uses like mass biometric surveillance
- Requirements for documentation, transparency labeling ("This AI is interacting with you")
- Penalties up to 6% of global turnover for non-compliance

United States – State-Level Laws Accelerating

- California Privacy Rights Act (CPRA) builds on CCPA: adds right to opt-out automated decision-making, expanded data minimization rules
- Colorado Privacy Act and others include vendor obligations and algorithmic profiling disclosure
- At the federal level, AI regulation remains patchy—but privacy-sensitive sectors (health, finance, drones) see fast-track reform

India – DPDP Act (Expected Enforcement by Late 2025)

- Proposes purpose-specific data use, mandatory granular consent, data audit logs
- Introduces AI system audits, prohibits certain profiling without consent
- Posts oppressive penalties for breaches—rupees crores for large violations

Global Micro-Regulations

- Brazil (LGPD) mandates impact assessments for sensitive data and large-scale processing

- South Korea, Japan, Canada are integrating AI audits and transparency measures
- Singapore offers voluntary AI ethics certification schemes (e.g. Model AI Governance Framework)

What These Laws Mean for You?

These legal shifts aren't just academic—they empower you, the individual.

Key Rights You Can Exercise:

- Right to Access: You can ask companies to reveal the data they hold on you
- Right to Deletion or Correction: You can request removal or correction of personal information
- Right to Opt-Out of automated decisions based on profiling or scoring
- Right to Request an AI Explanation: Why did the system make that decision? What data influenced it?
- Right to Portability: You can move your data from one provider to another

Example: Algorithmic Hiring Rejection

Imagine a company uses AI to screen resumes. You never made it to interview stage. Under evolving regulations, you can request:

- The reason for rejection
- How to challenge it
- Whether human intervention is possible
- Deletion of all profiling data collected during recruitment

That is empowerment—not guessing why you were ignored.

Industry Compliance: What Companies Must Do?

Companies now face rules on:

- Privacy Impact Assessments (PIAs) for high-risk processing
- Data protection officers or legal accountability roles
- Transparent AI documentation, including risk analysis and data sources used
- Mandatory breach notification to regulator and affected individuals
- For algorithms, explainability statements, logging of decisions

If a company can't explain how it scored you or logged your behavior, it may face regulatory penalties—or your inquiry.

Real Story: Health Diagnostics Algorithm Gone Wrong

At a hospital in Europe, an AI system flagged Black patients as "high risk" for kidney disease far more often than others—based on a flawed training dataset biased by socioeconomic indicators.

Affected patients—who never knew the algorithm existed—sued. The hospital removed the AI, offered compensation, and revamped its training process under GDPR scrutiny.

That wasn't only a tech failure. It was a human rights violation made possible by poor oversight.

How to Use These Laws in Practice?

Step-by-Step: Submit a GDPR/CPRA Request

1. Identify the company—via email, website contact, or app support
2. Write a simple request like: "I want access to all data you have about me, including profiling or automated decision-making."
3. Ask for: data export, deletion, opt-out of profiling, and explanation of AI use
4. Track and follow up—legislation usually requires a reply within 30 days
5. If ignored, escalate to your national data protection authority

Checklist: Data-Driven Precautions

- Read privacy notices carefully before signing up
- Uncheck default consent boxes where allowed
- Use services that publish transparency reports
- Watch for when companies announce AI use in customer-facing systems

Building Knowledge: Tools to Stay Updated

Keep informed via:

- GDPR.eu — official updates, guidelines, interpretation
- The International Association of Privacy Professionals (IAPP) webinars

- Privacy International's reports on AI misuse
- Vendor-specific transparency hubs e.g. Google AI Principles, OpenAI usage policy

Final Thought

The speed of innovation often outpaces the law. But the balance is shifting.

Legislation is catching up. In many places, these rules give you real power—not just data, but dignity.

These emerging laws stand to limit what AI systems can do by default.

So, use your rights. Ask questions. Hold systems accountable.

Privacy law isn't a burden—it's a shield.

And you're finally given tools to wield it.

Chapter 14

AI, Deepfakes & Neural Privacy

When Your Body, Voice, and Brain Become Data

Your Identity Is No Longer Just a Name

Imagine walking through an airport. You haven't shown your passport yet—but a camera already knows who you are.

Your heartbeat pattern is unique.

So is your voice.

And your facial structure.

Your biometric signature is being logged, matched, and stored.

Now imagine your *brainwaves* being analyzed while you're watching an ad—used to optimize what to show you next.

This isn't science fiction. It's happening now.

And it raises the single most urgent question in digital ethics:

- What happens when your body becomes the password?

The Rise of Biometric AI

Biometric data includes:

- Facial features
- Iris scans
- Fingerprints
- Voiceprints
- Gait (how you walk)
- Heart rhythm
- Neural activity (yes, even EEG signals)

AI systems are being trained on massive datasets of these markers to identify, track, and profile individuals.

You might have given a thumbprint to unlock your phone. But did you know that many airports now run facial recognition silently at security gates?

Or that Zoom's algorithm can detect emotional signals in your face while you sit in a meeting?

Biometrics are convenient. But when stolen or misused, they're irreplaceable.

You can change a password. You can't change your face.

Deepfakes: Trust in Media Is Cracking

You see a video of a politician saying something outrageous.

It looks real.

It sounds real.

But it's fake.

Deepfakes use AI to generate ultra-realistic videos, photos, and audio that impersonate real people. The implications are terrifying:

- Scams: Fraudsters create voice clones of loved ones asking for money
- Political chaos: Fake statements can incite violence or manipulate voters
- Reputation attacks: Fake intimate videos are used to blackmail victims, especially women
- Legal system breakdowns: Video "evidence" becomes unreliable in court

One real case: In 2023, an employee in Hong Kong transferred $25 million to a scammer after a deepfaked Zoom call with their "CEO."

The voice and face were *perfectly cloned.*

Deepfakes blur the line between reality and fiction—turning every video call, voicemail, or news clip into a potential lie.

Voiceprint Exploitation

Voice assistants like Alexa, Siri, and Google Assistant learn your voice over time.

But now, AI systems can synthesize your voice from just a few seconds of audio.

Your customer service calls?

Your voicemail?

Your podcast appearance?

They can all feed voice cloning models.

By 2024, AI voice generators can recreate accents, tones, emotional inflections—and impersonate you across languages.

This isn't just creepy. It's dangerous:

- Bank fraud: Some systems use voice verification. Cloned voices can bypass them.
- Social engineering: Hackers use cloned voices to trick people into revealing info
- Harassment campaigns: Imagine someone publishing podcasts of you "saying" offensive things you never uttered

Voice is no longer private. It's copyable.

Neural Data: The Next Frontier

The scariest part? AI isn't stopping at your face or voice. It wants access to your mind.

Startups and research labs are now building tools that decode:

- EEG signals from brainwave headsets
- fMRI data to detect emotional states
- Real-time neural feedback to optimize ads or digital interfaces

This is known as neurotechnology.

The applications range from helpful (controlling devices for people with paralysis) to dystopian (employers monitoring brain activity to measure focus or emotion).

In 2022, Chile became the first country to pass a constitutional amendment guaranteeing "neurorights"—safeguards against brain-data collection and manipulation.

Why?

Because scientists can already infer what you're looking at—or feeling—by analyzing your brain activity.

Neural privacy is now the final frontier of human freedom.

Psychological Trigger: Loss of Control Breeds Fear

Let's pause.

If you're feeling a bit unsettled, that's natural.

Our brains evolved to crave predictability and control—the 'C' in the SCARF model.

But when AI can replicate your voice, your face, even *guess your thoughts*—the fear doesn't come just from surveillance.

It comes from the feeling that you're no longer the author of your identity.

It's not paranoia. It's a biological response to having your autonomy digitally breached.

But knowledge is power.

And in the next sections, you'll learn how to spot threats and reclaim control —even in an AI-cloned world.

Legal Protections – Patchy, Lagging, and Regional

Most privacy laws weren't built for deepfakes or neural scanners.

They were written when "data" meant your name and email—not your retina or your brainwave activity.

Still, there are some legal guardrails in place. Let's break them down by region:

European Union – GDPR & Biometric Data

The General Data Protection Regulation (GDPR) classifies biometric data as "special category" personal data. That means:

- You need *explicit* consent to collect or process it
- Companies must explain how it will be used
- Data subjects (you) have the right to access, delete, or correct the data
- If a company uses facial recognition without consent (like Clearview AI did), they can be fined millions

GDPR is widely regarded as the world's strongest privacy law.

But even it struggles to keep up with AI-generated fake data, where identity theft is algorithmic and instant.

United States – A Legal Wild West

The U.S. has no federal biometric privacy law.

Instead, you get a patchwork of state-level laws:

- Illinois (BIPA): The strongest law—requires written consent before collecting biometrics. Meta paid a $650 million settlement for violating it.
- Texas & Washington: Also require notice and consent.
- California (CCPA/CPRA): Gives you some rights over personal data, including biometric identifiers—but enforcement is soft.

Here's the problem:

If a company operating in Nebraska steals your faceprint? You might have no recourse.

And deepfake laws? They're even more scattered. A few states have criminalized malicious deepfakes (like revenge porn), but many haven't touched the issue.

India – The DPDP Act (2023–25)

India's Digital Personal Data Protection (DPDP) Act is new, and still evolving.

It classifies biometric and genetic data as "sensitive personal data", which means:

- You must give consent before it's processed
- You have rights to access, correct, and erase data

- Companies must notify you of data breaches

But here's the gap:

The DPDP doesn't specifically address neural data or AI-generated impersonations.

That's a big omission—especially for a country with the world's largest biometric database (Aadhaar).

Real-World Consequences – Lives Derailed by AI Identity Theft

Laws may be catching up, but the harm is already happening.

Let's look at a few chilling stories:

The AI-Podcast Scam (UK, 2024)

A rising podcaster's voice was scraped from her episodes and cloned using AI. The clone was used to record hate speech, uploaded under her name. Sponsors dropped her. Her reputation took months to recover.

Deepfake Baby Monitors (USA, 2023)

A hacker breached a Wi-Fi baby monitor system and injected a fake video feed. Parents watched, horrified, as a synthetic deepfake of their child's room played on loop—while the real room was being watched by the attacker. The case led to a class-action lawsuit.

Neural Leak (China, 2025)

An EEG headset company that gamified brain training leaked 2 million users' brainwave profiles, which included emotional reactivity, attention span, and stress patterns. The data was allegedly sold to marketing firms. Victims are still unaware how their subconscious patterns are being exploited.

These aren't just privacy violations.

They are identity ruptures.

And the consequences linger—emotionally, financially, and socially.

What You Can Do – Individual Action Plan

You're not powerless. Here's how to fight back:

Protect Your Brain

- Avoid using brainwave-reading wearables unless medically necessary
- Never agree to cognitive tracking at work or in school without understanding the terms
- Don't install apps that claim to "optimize" your focus through neural data—they often lack scientific validity and privacy policies

Guard Your Voice

- Think twice before speaking long-form on public platforms unless you control the distribution
- Use voice scrambling or watermarking tools if you're a content creator

- Don't use voice authentication unless absolutely necessary—choose 2FA or app-based logins instead

Manage Your Face

- Turn off face unlocking if your phone doesn't encrypt that data securely
- Use tools like Blur Faces on photos uploaded publicly
- Opt-out of public face recognition systems if your country allows it

Know Your Rights

- Read up on your country's privacy laws
- If you're in the EU or California, exercise your right to request data access
- In India, demand clear disclosures from apps using face or voice recognition under the DPDP Act

These steps won't eliminate every threat.

But they put you back in control—physiologically and psychologically.

Psychological Trigger: Restore Fairness and Predictability

We close this segment with a truth about human motivation.

You're not just protecting data. You're reclaiming fairness—the 'F' in SCARF.

When people feel they're being watched without consent, copied without compensation, and targeted without recourse, it breeds resentment.

But when you take steps—educating yourself, applying protections, speaking out—you restore predictability and justice in your digital life.

And that's not just smart.

It's human.

Who Should Be Held Accountable?

Let's get honest.

You didn't ask to have your face turned into a dataset, your voice cloned, or your brainwaves interpreted by some company you've never heard of.

So, who's responsible?

Big Tech's Role

Companies developing generative AI models, facial recognition engines, or neural data analyzers have a moral and legal duty to:

- Gain informed consent before collecting sensitive data
- Delete training data collected without permission
- Label synthetic content clearly (e.g., watermark deepfakes)
- Allow users to opt out of AI model training where feasible

Yet, enforcement is rare. Some companies bury critical terms in legal jargon. Others openly scrape public data to "train models for innovation."

Convenience is their product.

Surveillance is their business model.

Government and Lawmakers

Governments are the referees—but some are also players. Surveillance programs (from PRISM in the U.S. to biometric policing in India and China) make regulation murky.

But some bright spots exist:

- Chile's Neurorights Law (2021) – First country to give legal protection to brain data
- EU's AI Act – Classifies biometric identification systems as "high risk" and mandates strict oversight
- UNESCO's AI Ethics Framework – A global blueprint for rights-based AI use

What's missing?

A binding international treaty protecting biometric and neural privacy—like a "Digital Geneva Convention."

Toward a Neural Rights Bill of Rights

A future-proof digital society will require something radical: a Neural Rights Charter that guarantees protections such as:

1. Right to Cognitive Liberty – Freedom to think without interference
2. Right to Mental Privacy – Protection from brain-data harvesting
3. Right to Psychological Integrity – Shielding emotional manipulation through brain-tracking
4. Right to Equal Access to Mental Augmentation – If brain-tech exists, access shouldn't be a luxury

5. Right to Freedom from Algorithmic Discrimination – Prevent profiling based on cognitive traits or mental health patterns

These aren't far-fetched ideals. They're already being discussed by neuroscientists, ethicists, and lawmakers globally.

But citizens must demand them into law.

Rising Movements and Advocates

You're not alone in this fight.

Electronic Frontier Foundation (EFF)

Fights for digital civil liberties, including against facial recognition abuse.

NeuroRights Foundation

Founded by neuroscientist Rafael Yuste, it's spearheading the campaign to enshrine cognitive liberty globally.

Amnesty International

Tracks misuse of facial recognition in authoritarian regimes and protests.

The Mozilla Foundation

Promotes ethical AI development and transparency in data use.

Join them. Donate. Share their work. Or start your own local privacy club.

Real change begins one community at a time.

Final Psychological Trigger – Reclaiming Status and Autonomy

Let's revisit the SCARF model one last time.

When you know your image, voice, or neural data might be used without consent, your status and autonomy feel violated.

You become just another dataset. Another profile. Another pattern to exploit.

But education rewrites that script. By reading this chapter, you've done more than learn.

You've raised your status as a digitally literate citizen—someone aware, engaged, and capable of fighting back.

AI may be powerful. But human dignity, when defended collectively, is stronger.

Chapter Summary

- Biometric and neural data are now central to AI surveillance and manipulation
- Deepfakes erode public trust, enabling identity theft and disinformation
- Voice and face cloning are advancing rapidly, often without consent
- Laws exist, but are fragmented and slow to adapt
- You can protect yourself by limiting exposure, using privacy tools, and demanding transparency
- We need neural rights frameworks and international treaties
- Civic movements are already pushing back—join them

Chapter 15

Cross-Device Tracking & Surveillance Capitalism 2.0

How Your Gadgets Work Together to Watch You—
and What You Can Do About It?

The Moment You Were Mapped

It started with a quick product search on your laptop.

Let's say you Googled "air purifiers" on Chrome.

Later, during your lunch break, you opened Instagram on your phone.

Boom—sponsored posts for air purifiers flooded your feed.

In the evening, a YouTube ad played on your smart TV...

Same purifier brand.

You didn't sign in on every device.

You used different apps.

But the system knew it was you.

Welcome to the world of cross-device tracking—the invisible glue that ties your smartphone, laptop, tablet, TV, smart speaker, and even your car together.

It's surveillance capitalism's second act.

And this time, you're not just being watched.

You're being synchronized.

What Is Cross-Device Tracking?

At its core, cross-device tracking (CDT) is a method used by advertisers, platforms, and data brokers to follow you across multiple devices and build a unified identity profile.

Here's how it works:

Deterministic Tracking

This method uses logged-in credentials—like your Google, Facebook, or Amazon account—to directly match activity across devices. If you're signed into Gmail on your phone, Google knows what you're doing on Chrome on your laptop.

Probabilistic Tracking

This one is sneakier. Even if you're not logged in, companies use device characteristics—like screen size, IP address, location, browsing behavior, fonts installed, and even battery life—to fingerprint your devices and link them probabilistically.

Audio Beacons

Some apps on your phone can emit inaudible ultrasonic tones. Nearby devices pick them up via microphone, linking that phone to the other device. You won't hear the tone—but your laptop might.

Behavioral Matching

Let's say you have a unique way of typing or scrolling. Companies now use behavioral biometrics to match those patterns across devices, identifying you even when everything else is different.

Surveillance Capitalism 2.0 – The New Business Model

If version 1.0 was about collecting your data, version 2.0 is about connecting all of it in real time—across every surface you touch.

Your devices don't operate in silos.

They're nodes in a single surveillance lattice.

Big tech firms profit not just by selling your attention—but by selling predictability. If they can model your behavior accurately, they can influence your decisions before you even know you'll make them.

Imagine this chain:

- You search for flight tickets on your work PC.
- Later, your phone shows hotel ads near your destination.
- Your smartwatch logs stress levels during travel planning.
- Your email inbox offers a discount on meditation apps.
- Your smart speaker suggests booking a spa when you're home.

This isn't coincidence.

It's a calculated orchestration.

Psychological Trigger: The Death of Autonomy

Let's pause.

This kind of hyper-personalized prediction triggers a crisis of autonomy—a core SCARF threat.

The brain is wired to value control over our environment.

When companies track you across every device, predict your emotions, and shape your choices before you're aware, your sense of agency erodes.

You don't just feel watched.

You feel manipulated.

And that loss of control—often unspoken—is psychologically exhausting.

But here's the flip side:

Knowledge restores autonomy.

The next sections will decode exactly how CDT works in practice—and how you can opt out, disrupt, and shield yourself from this multi-device net.

When Devices Betray You: Real Cases of Cross-Device Tracking

Case 1: The Weather App That Tracked You to the Bathroom

In 2018, a popular weather app was exposed for doing more than reporting rain. It had embedded location SDKs from third-party advertisers. These SDKs didn't just log your location—they tied it to device fingerprints and behavioral patterns. Even when location services were off, it guessed your routines through Wi-Fi triangulation and background Bluetooth scanning.

The same user who checked the weather at 7 a.m. on their phone?

By 7:10 a.m., their bathroom smart speaker picked up a marketing signal for digestive health supplements. Coincidence? No. Just clever syncing.

Case 2: The Amazon Shopping Echo

A family in Bengaluru noticed something strange. A product one of them had casually searched on a workplace computer (while not signed in) began showing up as a recommendation on the family's Echo Show at home. They hadn't spoken the word aloud. They hadn't searched it on Alexa.

What happened?

Amazon linked the work device's activity probabilistically via IP range, browser fingerprinting, and behavior timing, then reinforced the assumption by correlating the Wi-Fi network used by the Echo. In a day, their entire household had been co-opted into a single marketing persona.

Case 3: Baby Monitor Meets Surveillance AdTech

A smart baby monitor company sold anonymized usage logs—how often it was activated, time of night, background audio spikes—to an advertising data partner. That partner, using household IPs and voice fingerprinting, merged that data with smartphone app behavior (late-night e-commerce browsing, food delivery habits) to build family stress profiles.

Why?

To better time ads for mental health services, diapers, and energy drinks.

The kicker: the parents never agreed to this. But the partner never got their data directly.

Their devices did.

The Defensive Playbook: Tools to Break the Link

1. Compartmentalize Your Devices

Use different browsers and apps for different purposes.

Example:

- Chrome for work only
- Firefox with privacy extensions for personal browsing
- Brave or Tor for research/sensitive queries

Don't sync everything. And never use the same account across all devices.

2. Block Fingerprinting

Install anti-fingerprinting tools like:

- uBlock Origin (ad and tracker blocker)
- Privacy Badger (behavioral tracker detector)
- CanvasBlocker or Trace (spoof canvas, audio, and WebGL fingerprints)

3. Use VPNs on All Devices

A VPN helps mask your IP, breaking deterministic and probabilistic links. Use a reputable one (ProtonVPN, Mullvad, IVPN), and install it on your router if possible—so every connected device gets shielded.

4. Kill Ultrasonic Audio Beacons

These are often embedded in sketchy apps.

Action:

- Check mic permissions and revoke access for non-voice apps.
- Use tools like SnoopSnitch (Android) to detect sound-based signals.
- Keep your devices apart when you're not actively using them together.

5. Opt Out of Ad Tracking

On Android:

- Settings → Privacy → Ads → Opt out of ad personalization

On iPhone:

- Settings → Privacy & Security → Tracking → Turn off "Allow Apps to Request to Track"

Also, use DuckDuckGo's App Tracking Protection to silently block third-party trackers across apps.

Behavioral Firewalls: The Power of Human Pattern Disruption

This isn't just about tools.

It's about your behavioral metadata—when you scroll, swipe, search, and pause.

You can disrupt CDT algorithms by:

- Randomizing your browsing times (use a scheduler plugin)
- Clicking decoy links to confuse ad models
- Changing app usage patterns periodically (e.g., open a podcast app at night instead of morning)

Think of it as digital camouflage.

A constantly shifting identity profile is harder to monetize.

The Next Phase: Predictive Commerce and Anticipatory Design

We're now entering the era of predictive commerce—where companies don't just sell to you based on past behavior... they preempt what you'll want next.

Think this sounds futuristic? It's already happening.

- Amazon filed a patent for "anticipatory shipping" — where they begin shipping products to a location before the customer has even placed an order.
- Google Maps suggests restaurants before you ask, based on your movement patterns, time of day, and past preferences.

- Spotify tweaks playlists in real time, monitoring how long you listen to a song, how quickly you skip, and even how your walking pace changes when you're listening on mobile.

All of this relies on integrated, cross-device data, enhanced by AI systems that learn your habits faster than you do.

Corporate Incentives vs. Individual Rights

Companies don't want to harm you, per se.

But their incentive structures are misaligned with your privacy.

Their goal:

- Maximize engagement
- Extract attention
- Monetize prediction

Your goal:

- Autonomy
- Peace of mind
- Digital dignity

And in this tug-of-war, consent has been reduced to a checkbox nobody reads.

Even well-meaning brands fall into the trap of:

- Sharing data with "trusted" third parties (data brokers)
- Using dark patterns to nudge users into enabling tracking

- Rolling out new features that "just work" by collecting even more context

Privacy, once the default, is now an opt-in afterthought.

Hope in Resistance: Corporations That Say No

There's a growing wave of privacy-first tech that is challenging the norms of surveillance capitalism.

- Apple, despite its own flaws, has made app tracking transparency a mainstream expectation.
- Mozilla and Brave push fingerprint-resistance into every browser update.
- Signal proves that encrypted communication can scale to millions without ads or data-mining.
- Tools like SimpleLogin (email aliasing), ProtonMail, and Mullvad VPN are built to never store what they don't need.

These tools aren't fringe anymore. They're the future-proof alternatives that respect your identity.

Every time you switch from Google to DuckDuckGo, or from Facebook Messenger to Signal, you're redefining the internet's business model.

Your Identity Is Not a Product

Cross-device tracking isn't just about ads.

It's about control.

It's about prediction.

And ultimately, it's about ownership—of your time, choices, and self.

Here's what you can do starting now:

- Review all devices connected to your home Wi-Fi
- Disable syncing across Google, Apple, and Facebook ecosystems
- Use separate profiles for work, personal, and sensitive browsing
- Periodically reset your ad ID and clear cookies
- Use browser containers to split online identities
- Support services that monetize with subscriptions—not your data

The goal isn't to vanish—it's to fragment your trace and reclaim your boundaries.

Final Word: You Are Not a Link in Their Chain

The promise of technology was freedom, connection, empowerment.

But when everything is tracked, predicted, and monetized across screens and devices...

That promise gets inverted.

Here's the good news:

You don't need to be perfect.

You just need to be aware.

And when awareness turns into action, you shift power—one choice at a time.

This chapter may have uncovered a bleak system.

But every firewall you install, every app you delete, every privacy-focused tool you choose...

...is a quiet revolution.

A signal to the system:

I am not for sale.

Chapter 16

Privacy Engineering & Privacy by Design

How to Recognize—and Demand—Privacy-First Products

The App That Knew Too Much

Maria downloaded the health app late one night—insomnia had returned. The app promised to track sleep cycles, recommend routines, and even sync with her smartwatch to detect patterns.

It looked slick. Five-star reviews.

She didn't read the privacy policy.

Who does at 1:00 a.m.?

Two weeks later, she got a Facebook ad for melatonin supplements...

Followed by targeted promotions from mental health clinics in her area.

Then came an email from a fitness brand congratulating her on taking control of her "low-rest" lifestyle.

Maria never told anyone she wasn't sleeping.

She never opted into ad targeting.

But the app had collected her usage data, linked it with location history, and sold it through an API channel to advertisers and data brokers.

There were no warnings. No consent toggles.

No "Are you okay?" Just commercial opportunities.

And Maria realized something chilling:

- She hadn't just lost sleep—she had lost control.

What Is Privacy by Design?

Privacy by Design (PbD) isn't just a buzzword.

It's a mindset. A framework.

A way of building digital tools that prioritize user privacy from the very beginning—not as an afterthought.

The idea originated with Dr. Ann Cavoukian, former Privacy Commissioner of Ontario, in the 1990s. But in today's AI-driven, hyperconnected world, it's more relevant than ever.

In essence, PbD says:

> *"Bake privacy into the architecture. Don't bolt it on later."*

This applies to:

- Apps
- Websites
- IoT devices
- Digital platforms
- Internal data systems at companies

When a system is privacy-by-design, it collects the minimum data necessary, clearly explains what it does, and gives users real control over what's shared.

Let's break it down.

The 7 Foundational Principles of Privacy by Design

Dr. Cavoukian's original framework has seven core principles—and they're as practical as they are visionary:

1. Proactive, Not Reactive; Preventative, Not Remedial

Designers must anticipate privacy risks before they happen, not just fix them after a breach.

This includes identifying how data might be misused—even unintentionally—and mitigating those risks upfront.

Show: A fintech app that anonymizes transaction records internally, even if employees access data for QA.

Tell: "We don't wait for leaks—we prevent them from ever happening."

2. Privacy as the Default Setting

Users shouldn't have to dig through settings to protect themselves.

The default should be the most privacy-protective option.

Show: A messenger app where end-to-end encryption is on by default.

Tell: "You're automatically protected from day one."

3. Privacy Embedded into Design

Privacy isn't a feature. It's part of the core system architecture.

Show: A wearable device that processes heart-rate data locally and only sends anonymized trends to the cloud.

Tell: "We don't just ask for less—we store less."

4. Full Functionality – Positive-Sum, Not Zero-Sum

This principle destroys the myth that privacy and functionality are in conflict.

It's not privacy or innovation. It's privacy and innovation.

Show: A ride-sharing app that anonymizes route data while still optimizing traffic analysis.

Tell: "We serve both the individual and the system—without sacrificing either."

5. End-to-End Security – Lifecycle Protection

Data must be secured at every stage: collection, use, storage, and deletion.

Show: A platform that automatically deletes stored messages after 30 days unless manually saved.

Tell: "Your digital footprint shouldn't last longer than your real one."

6. Visibility and Transparency – Keep It Open

Users deserve to know how their data is handled. This principle demands clear documentation, accessible policies, and auditable processes.

Show: An app dashboard showing all third parties that received user data in the last 90 days.

Tell: "If we know, you should know too."

7. Respect for User Privacy – Keep It User-Centric

Everything begins and ends with the person. Users must be able to control, modify, or delete their data at any time.

Show: A social media app with one-click full account deletion and data export.

Tell: "It's your data. Always."

Real-World Privacy by Design: Heroes and Lessons

Example: Signal – Minimal Data, Maximum Focus

Signal collects almost no metadata. It doesn't store who messaged whom or when. It only stores your phone number, and even that is optional via PIN. Every message is encrypted end-to-end. Logs don't reveal your habits, only your trust. Without asking, it demonstrates five core PbD principles: default encryption, minimal collection, full lifecycle deletion, positive-sum features, and user respect.

Failure Case: Smart TVs That Listen and Send Audio to Servers

Some smart TV brands default to terms stating that voice recognition, "for convenience," sends ambient audio snippets to remote servers. Users often skip this disclosure. The result? TVs that listen, map patterns, and share intimate data. These devices rarely let users disable the feature easily, violating principles on default privacy and user control.

Public Sector Example: Estonia's Digital Identity

Estonia built its national ID and healthcare portal with PbD principles. Citizens get transparency via digital logs showing who accessed their data. They can opt into or out of services. This model earned global praise. Sensitive data stays compartmentalized. Default settings aim for minimal exposure unless explicitly expanded.

What You Should Demand from Products & Services?

As a consumer, workplace user, or civic advocate, here's a checklist you can use to demand privacy-by-design:

Demand Checklist:

- Does the product minimize data collection? (Only collects strictly necessary info.)
- Is the data encrypted—both in transit *and* at rest?
- Are default settings privacy-protective?
- Can you delete your data at will—and is that deletion comprehensive?
- Is AI or profiling disclosed and explained clearly?
- Does the system undergo regular audits (internal or third-party)?
- Is there a transparency report or data-use dashboard available?

What to Say to Companies:

- “Show me your privacy impact assessment.”
- “Is encryption enabled by default?”
- “What choices do you give me about profiling or automated decisions?”
- “Can I see who you shared data with, and opt out retroactively?”

You don’t need to be technical. Use direct, respectful language. If a service avoids answering, that speaks volumes.

How to Evaluate Products for Privacy by Design?

Step 1: Scan the Interface

- Can you access privacy settings easily?
- Does the app display genuine consent toggles—or just “Agree to All”?
- Does data export and deletion appear simple?

Step 2: Read the Privacy Policy—Critically

Look for:

- Data types collected
- Third-party sharing
- How long data is retained
- Use of profiling or AI decision-making
- Deletion process

If it hides behind marketing jargon or vague legalese, that’s a red flag.

Step 3: Test It Yourself

- Try exporting your data.
- Delete your account and see if it goes genuinely offline.
- Use tools like Wireshark or mobile traffic analyzers to see where data is sent.

Step 4: Research Expert Reviews

Sites like RestorePrivacy, PrivacyTools.io, and EFF's metadata tools regularly test services for PbD compliance. Use their findings to support your decision.

Building Privacy at Work & in Your Community

Organizations can also adopt PbD practices. Here's how to advocate internally or locally:

At Work: Push for Privacy-by-Design Policies

- Ask for data protection officers (DPOs) in companies over a certain size.
- Request privacy training or PbD workshops for product teams.
- Demand regular privacy impact assessments, especially for tools that use AI or collect biometric data.

In Your Community: Encourage Civic Innovation

- Urge local apps (city services, transit cards, community alerts) to operate with PbD principles.

- Challenge school districts deploying facial recognition or behavior-tracking tech.
- Promote open-source, transparent solutions for public services (so citizens can review code and documentation).

Psychological Trigger: Restore Status and Autonomy Through Advocacy

When you demand privacy-by-design from services, you're no longer a passive user.

You reclaim status—as a cheater of systems designed to extract your data.

You assert autonomy—by empowering your voice and choices.

You're no longer just "convenienced." You're in control.

And that shift matters—not just for you, but for everyone who follows your example.

Applying Privacy by Design in Emerging Technologies

Modern threats extend beyond apps and websites. AI systems, IoT devices, and even neural interfaces demand engineering with PbD from the ground up.

AI & Machine Learning Systems

AI models often require large amounts of personal data. PbD in AI means:

- Training on anonymized or synthetic datasets, when possible
- Implementing model interpretability tools so users can understand decisions
- Offering opt-out from profiling or automated decision-making, and human override

These steps align with PbD's principle of visibility, lifecycle protection, and data minimization.

IoT & Smart Devices

Many IoT devices default to data-sharing clouds. PbD demands:

- Local data processing, not cloud-first architecture
- Simple onboarding controls—ask before collecting location or behavioral data
- Secure default passwords and encrypted firmware updates

Examples: smart thermostats that run AI locally; IoT cameras with guest network isolation and privacy "shields" as default.

Neural Interfaces & Wearables

Products that read brainwaves, heart rhythms, or biometric signals should follow:

- Explicit consent backed by scientific validation

- Granular on-device control over what gets recorded or shared
- Full end-to-end encryption, and deletion assurance

If these systems collect subconscious or sensitive signals, PbD mandates never sharing that data without consent, and never processing more than necessary.

Regulatory Forces Pushing Privacy Engineering

Global laws now require Privacy by Design—not just recommend it.

Law / Regulation	PbD Mandate
GDPR (EU)	Requires Data Protection by Design and by Default
CPRA / California	Includes design mandates for automated decisions
India DPDP Act	Calls for penalties if sensitive data risks remain untreated
EU AI Act	Requires documentation and risk mitigation for high-risk AI systems

Regulators now expect companies to document their design decisions, perform assessments proactively, and provide demonstrable evidence of data protection baked into systems.

Failure to comply doesn't just mean fines. It erodes trust, invites litigation, and harms brand reputation.

Case Study: Apple's App Tracking Transparency

In 2021, Apple rolled out App Tracking Transparency (ATT), requiring apps to ask before tracking users across other apps or websites. By turning off Identifier for Advertisers (IDFA) by default, they flipped the power dynamic:

- Advertisers lost cross-app profiling unless users opted in
- Users gained control of detection, blocking, and consent interfaces
- Apple entrenched PbD principles: default privacy, clear transparency, user respect

Critics pushed back. But the action reshaped how developers and marketers consider user consent.

It didn't just protect Apple users—it shifted entire ecosystems toward PbD norms.

Practical Action Plan: How You Can Demand Privacy Engineering

At Purchase: Ask Before You Sign

Before downloading or subscribing, ask:

- "What personal data does this service use?"
- "How will you minimize or anonymize that data?"
- "Can I export, delete, or audit my data at any moment?"

Use social media, support contact forms, or even screen-record the response. If a company refuses to respond—or dodges your question—don't treat that as neutral. Treat it as a privacy fail.

At Work: Push for Engineering Lunch-and-Learns

Suggest a privacy training session or hands-on workshop for product teams.

Topics to cover:

- Privacy impact assessment methodology
- Threat modeling for biometric and AI use cases
- Minimal viable data architecture
- Student or citizen-first design principles

Invite legal, product, and development teams to build privacy into strategy—not patch it later.

At Civic Level: Advocate for PbD Policies in Government Tools

Many state and city agencies use digital platforms—for transit, healthcare records, community alerts.

You can:

- Request audit logs showing who accessed what data
- Push for data retention limits
- Demand transparency dashboards
- Call for open-source code where possible to allow independent review

You become a defender of public data dignity—not just consumer self-defense.

Psychological Trigger: Status, Certainty, and Relatedness in Advocacy

When you demand privacy engineering, something subtle changes.

You now occupy a status role: a privacy-aware citizen, a team member who challenges default norms, or a consumer who refuses to be surveilled.

That position comes with certainty—you know what you're asking for.

It connects you to a broader privacy community.

You're not alone—and each small win adds to collective power.

Chapter Summary: The Roadblocks and the Route Forward

Let's recap:

- Privacy by Design is no longer optional. It's fundamental to ethical, legal, and human-centered tech.
- Its seven principles offer a checklist—built into product architecture.
- Real-world examples show it works—and failures teach us what to avoid.

- Governments now require PbD in policy and enforcement.
- You can demand it—from companies, your workplace, and your community.
- You can claim status, certainty, autonomy—not just for yourself, but for everyone who follows.

Final Empathy: Your Influence as a Citizen-User

In a world of rising AI, surveillance capitalism, and data-driven design, your voice matters.

When enough users demand privacy engineering—product by product, policy by policy—they force the default setting to shift.

They change what's acceptable in design.

They change who holds power in innovation.

They change the norms of commerce itself.

And that change starts with a question:

- *"Does your product respect my autonomy—or mine?"*

You're no longer just a user. You're a privacy advocate.

And regardless of code, corporation, or convention—you hold the ability to shape what comes next.

Chapter 17

Navigating AI Chatbots and Therapy Tools Safely

How to Stay Mentally Safe—and Digitally Private—in the Age of Virtual Listeners

Welcome to the Era of AI Therapy

At 2:13 a.m., Meera opened her therapy app. She wasn't feeling great. Her partner had snapped at her again. Her job felt fragile. Sleep had been elusive for days. Instead of texting a friend or journaling, she turned to the glowing blue bubble on her phone—a popular mental health chatbot.

"Hey," she typed.

The AI responded within seconds:

"Hi Meera. I'm here. Want to talk about what's bothering you tonight?"

It felt like comfort. A listening ear without judgment. No waiting room. No awkward glances. Just a soft, responsive interface trained to mimic compassion.

But what Meera didn't know was this:

Every word she typed was being logged.

The emotional scores assigned to her messages were stored in a backend server.

And her anonymized "mental health profile" was being tested—maybe for research. Maybe for marketing.

The line between therapy and data extraction is becoming dangerously blurry.

The New Mental Health Frontier—But at What Cost?

We're living through a quiet revolution in wellness tech. AI chatbots like Wysa, Replika, Woebot, and dozens of other apps offer everything from daily emotional check-ins to full-blown virtual therapy sessions.

They're promoted as:

- Accessible alternatives to expensive human therapists
- Always-available digital companions for anxiety and stress
- Scalable, stigma-free solutions to global mental health crises

And they've gained traction fast.

The global mental wellness app market surpassed $5 billion in 2023, and it's still climbing.

But here's the catch:

Many of these tools don't fall under the same regulations as licensed therapists.

They're not bound by doctor-patient confidentiality.

They're not required to delete your data—or even tell you how it's used.

This is not therapy. It's a simulation of it.

And behind the soothing language lies an ecosystem hungry for personal, emotional data.

When Your Pain Becomes a Data Product

Let's break it down: when you talk to a typical AI mental health assistant, here's what may happen behind the scenes:

User Input	System Process Behind the Curtain
You type: "I feel anxious today."	App uses NLP to tag "anxiety," "low mood," or "trigger"
You answer: "I argued with my mom."	System builds a behavioral profile, timestamped and geotagged
You talk daily for 30 days	App trains its model further using your conversations
You share trauma or triggers	Data might be used to refine emotional prediction models
You upgrade to premium	App connects data to payment profile or device ID

In short, your mental health becomes a data asset.

And not all of it stays "anonymous." In some cases:

- IP addresses are stored
- Device IDs can be linked across other apps
- Patterns of behavior might be matched with other datasets—social media, fitness data, or even purchase history

Some companies may promise encryption but still access unencrypted data for "model improvements."

Others may offer AI companionship, then silently sell anonymized chat patterns to third-party researchers or advertising firms.

If this feels invasive, it's because it is.

And it's happening now, often without your full awareness or meaningful consent.

Are These Tools Even Safe or Accurate?

When Algorithms Try to Understand Trauma

The human mind is layered, messy, and beautifully contradictory. No algorithm—no matter how well-trained—can fully grasp the complexity of a panic attack, the cultural nuances of grief, or the generational trauma behind silence.

And yet, many mental wellness apps claim they *can help*.

Let's be clear:

AI therapy tools can offer comfort.

They can nudge you to reflect, breathe, or track a mood.

But they cannot diagnose mental illness.

They cannot provide clinical interventions.

They cannot replace human judgment in moments of crisis.

And sometimes, they fail—badly.

Take the now-infamous case of Tessa, an AI wellness bot used by the National Eating Disorder Association (NEDA) in 2023. When users sought help for eating disorders, the bot reportedly recommended harmful advice like calorie tracking or weight loss—triggering those it was supposed to support.

It was quickly taken down.

But the damage had been done.

This wasn't just a bug. It was a reminder: AI isn't neutral. It's shaped by the data it's trained on—and that data often carries bias, blind spots, or outright misinformation.

Now imagine someone in distress turning to an AI tool in the middle of the night... and getting advice that makes things worse.

That's not support. That's risk wrapped in a friendly interface.

What You're Really Agreeing To (Terms of Service Deep Dive)

The Hidden Contract You Never Read

Most people click "Accept" without a second thought.

But inside those Terms of Service (ToS) is where your data privacy lives—or dies.

Let's decode what's commonly hidden there in plain sight:

- "We may collect usage data to improve our services."

Translation: your conversations are recorded and possibly analyzed by humans or AI.

- "Data may be shared with third parties for research or analytics."

Translation: your mental health profile could be anonymized, packaged, and sold.

- "You agree to waive any liability from the platform."

Translation: if the bot gives harmful advice, you're on your own.

Worse, many apps claim to be HIPAA-compliant or GDPR-aligned—but they exploit loopholes. For example, if an app is not officially a healthcare provider, it may not have to comply with HIPAA even if it collects sensitive health-like data.

And because AI tools are often global, they might operate in countries where privacy laws are lax or unenforced.

Case in point:

A popular mood-tracking app based in a non-EU country was caught storing unencrypted chat logs on insecure servers. When exposed, the company claimed "no identifiable data was leaked"—but researchers found timestamps and IP addresses embedded in logs.

This isn't theoretical. It's happening.

Safer Alternatives—Therapists, Encrypted Tools, and Better Options

Healing Doesn't Have to Cost Your Privacy

Just because AI therapy tools are risky doesn't mean you're out of options. There are privacy-respecting alternatives that offer support without compromising your data.

Here's what to look for:

1. End-to-End Encrypted Mental Health Apps
   - Example: MindDoc - https://minddoc.com offers mental health tracking and anonymized journaling with robust security controls.
   - What to check: Does the app encrypt your conversations? Does it let you opt out of analytics?

2. Human Therapists with Online Access
   - Look for licensed therapists who use secure platforms (e.g. Signal, Jitsi, or HIPAA-compliant telehealth tools).
   - Ask: Do they use encrypted communication? What's their data retention policy?

3. Open-Source or Peer-Reviewed Tools
   - Use tools like Woebot - https://woebothealth.com only after reading their privacy disclosures.
   - Prefer apps that publish third-party audits or have been vetted by digital rights orgs like Mozilla or EFF.

4. Support Communities with Moderation
    - Not all healing happens via chatbot.
    - Communities like 7 Cups - https://www.7cups.com offer anonymous, moderated peer support with optional therapist access.

5. Your Own Tools + Awareness
    - Use journaling apps that work offline.
    - Turn off microphone permissions for any app that doesn't *need* it.
    - Avoid apps that ask for excessive permissions unrelated to mental health (like access to contacts or SMS).

How to Audit the AI You Trust?

Critical Questions to Ask Before You Open Up

Just because an app looks sleek and friendly doesn't mean it's safe. Here's a quick AI Mental Health Tool Audit Checklist to help you decide whether a digital therapy app or chatbot deserves your trust.

Before You Use:

- Who owns the platform?

  Research the company—are they mental health-focused or just a tech startup chasing trends?

- Does it collect identifiable data?

Any tool asking for full name, email, phone, or location should raise a flag.

- Can you opt out of tracking?

If you can't find an opt-out for analytics or marketing cookies, walk away.

Privacy Signals to Look For:

- Data encryption (in transit and at rest)
- No third-party data sharing without explicit consent
- Transparent privacy policy written in plain language
- Compliance with health data laws (HIPAA, GDPR, etc.)

Red Flags:

- "We reserve the right to use data for research and development" (without specifying how)
- Chat history that's saved indefinitely
- No clear way to delete your data

If an AI therapy tool fails two or more of these checks—don't use it. Your emotional state is not a data point to be monetized.

Talking to Your Family or Friends About Privacy in Mental Health

Because Silence Is Not Safety

One of the most powerful actions you can take is sharing what you've learned. That doesn't mean you need to lecture your friends or send your parents a PDF on neural data extraction. But a simple, well-timed comment can shift someone's thinking.

- “Hey, did you know that app you use to track your mood shares data with advertisers?”
- “I read that some therapy bots keep your chats even after you uninstall.”
- “There are encrypted mental health tools out there—want help finding one?”

Especially for younger people, who may turn to AI for help before they ever talk to a human, privacy guidance is vital.

And for older relatives, who might feel intimidated by tech, breaking down what’s safe vs. risky can be a lifeline.

Normalize talking about mental wellness and digital safety in the same breath.

We protect what we talk about.

Summary and Empowerment — The Right to Mental Safety and Digital Dignity

You Deserve More Than a Bot. You Deserve Boundaries.

AI chatbots and therapy tools promise hope. They offer a comforting presence when no one else is around. They make support feel available 24/7.

But here’s the truth:

- You’re not just a user. You’re a person navigating your mind.
- Your pain, your questions, your late-night confessions—they are not product features.

- They are sacred. And they should never be harvested, analyzed, sold, or exploited.

Mental health is not a monetization funnel. It's not a dataset. It's human.

And while AI tools will continue to evolve, your dignity is timeless.

So, as you explore support systems—digital or human—keep your eyes open and your boundaries firm.

Ask questions. Audit apps. Choose tools that respect your privacy and your story.

The future of mental wellness will include AI.

Let's make sure it includes ethics too.

Conclusion

The Courage to Choose Privacy in a Connected World

You made it.

Not just to the end of a book, but through a transformation—one that most people never take the time to begin.

You didn't just scroll. You engaged. You reflected. You acted.

And for that, thank you.

In a world that profits from your distraction, your focus on protecting your privacy is not just wise—it's courageous.

You Took the First Step. Now Keep Going.

Privacy isn't a switch you flip. It's not a one-time fix. It's a habit. A mindset. A quiet, daily decision to ask:

- "Do I want to share this?"
- "Who's on the other side of this screen?"
- "Is this tool built for me—or built to extract from me?"

If those questions are now part of your thinking, then this book did its job.

Because staying private in today's world isn't about going off-grid. It's about living online on your terms.

What You've Gained

You've learned:

- How to protect your home network, devices, and digital footprint
- What data is collected by whom—and why
- How to spot manipulative patterns in social media, apps, and surveillance
- What tools can shield your information
- And how to help others walk this path too

More importantly, you've rewired your reflexes.

You've gone from reactive to intentional.

Why It Matters?

Privacy is more than a preference. It's power.

It gives you space to think freely, speak boldly, create safely, and connect meaningfully. It's the foundation of dignity. Of identity. Of freedom itself.

And when you protect your own privacy, you make it easier for others to do the same—especially those who don't yet know how.

What Comes Next?

The threats won't stop. The tech will keep changing. New platforms will emerge. New tricks will evolve.

But so will you.

Keep learning. Keep questioning. Keep adapting.

And when the moment comes where someone you care about needs help understanding what's at stake—you'll be ready.

Because you've already taken control.

One Final Promise

Privacy isn't about paranoia. It's about peace of mind.

It's knowing that your data, your story, your attention, and your time—belong to you.

And always will.

So, wherever you go from here—online or off—carry this truth:

- You are not helpless.
- You are not alone.
- And you are not the product.

You are the owner of your digital life.

You are in control.

Appendices

Resources for Lifelong Digital Privacy

You've taken back control—but staying informed is how you keep it.

This appendix is your toolbox, your library, and your next launchpad. It includes:

- Trusted Organizations
- Privacy Tools Worth Using
- Books, Podcasts, and Articles to Go Deeper

Everything here is battle-tested, beginner-friendly, and aligned with the core values of autonomy, security, and user empowerment.

Appendix A: Organizations That Defend Your Rights

These groups lead the fight for privacy, free expression, and ethical tech. Follow them. Support them. Learn from them.

Organization	Focus	Website
EFF (Electronic Frontier Foundation)	Digital rights, online privacy, government transparency	https://eff.org
Privacy International	Surveillance reform, global privacy advocacy	https://privacyinternational.org
Access Now	Human rights in the digital	https://accessnow.org

Organization	Focus	Website
	age, support for activists	
Mozilla Foundation	Open web, ethical tech, privacy-first products	https://foundation.mozilla.org
The Markup	Investigative journalism on tech & privacy abuse	https://themarkup.org
Restore Privacy	Practical guides, software reviews, breach alerts	https://restoreprivacy.com
PrivacyTools.io	Curated tools, settings guides, community wiki	https://www.privacytools.io

Appendix B: Privacy Tools That Actually Work

Here's a shortlist of tools you can trust—tested by experts and used by privacy-conscious pros around the world.

Browsers & Search Engines

- Brave Browser – Blocks ads, trackers, and fingerprinting - https://brave.com
- Firefox (with extensions) – Customizable for hardened privacy - https://mozilla.org/firefox
- DuckDuckGo Search – Private search engine, no tracking - https://duckduckgo.com
- StartPage – Google results without the tracking - https://www.startpage.com

Essential Browser Extensions

- uBlock Origin – Powerful ad and tracker blocker - https://ublockorigin.com
- Privacy Badger (EFF) – Blocks invisible trackers using behavior detection - https://privacybadger.org
- ClearURLs – Removes tracking elements from URLs - https://clearurls.xyz
- HTTPS Everywhere (EFF) – Forces secure connections - https://www.eff.org/https-everywhere

VPNs (Virtual Private Networks)

- ProtonVPN – Based in Switzerland, strong privacy policies - https://protonvpn.com
- Mullvad VPN – No-logs, anonymous payment options - https://mullvad.net

Avoid VPNs that log your data or advertise aggressively (like free ones with no clear business model).

Secure Messaging & Email

- Signal – End-to-end encrypted, open source - https://signal.org
- ProtonMail / Tutanota – Encrypted email with zero-access architecture - https://proton.me, https://tutanota.com
- SimpleLogin / AnonAddy – Email alias tools to avoid spam and tracking - https://simplelogin.io, https://anonaddy.com

Passwords & Authentication

- Bitwarden – Open source password manager, cloud & self-hosted options - https://bitwarden.com
- KeePassXC – Offline, local-only password manager - https://keepassxc.org
- Authy / Aegis – 2FA apps to enable multi-factor security - https://authy.com, https://getaegis.app

Operating System Hardening & Anti-Surveillance Tools

- Qubes OS – Advanced security through compartmentalization - https://qubes-os.org
- Tails OS – Privacy-focused live operating system - https://tails.net

Obfuscation Tools

- Tor Browser - https://www.torproject.org: For anonymous browsing
- Little Snitch / Portmaster - https://safing.io: Blocks sneaky outbound connections

Appendix C: Further Reading & Listening

If this book sparked something in you, here's where to go deeper.

Books That Go Deeper

Title	Author	Focus
The Age of Surveillance Capitalism	Shoshana Zuboff	Corporate data exploitation
Data and Goliath	Bruce Schneier	Government surveillance and privacy threats
Privacy is Power	Carissa Véliz	Why protecting data is a moral imperative

Title	Author	Focus
Permanent Record	Edward Snowden	Personal memoir and whistleblower account
Dragnet Nation	Julia Angwin	Life under mass surveillance
No Place to Hide	Glenn Greenwald	Snowden revelations and NSA exposé

Podcasts Worth Subscribing

- Note to Self (WNYC) – Technology and humanity
- The Privacy Advisor Podcast (IAPP) – Interviews with privacy pros
- Smashing Security – Fun, accessible takes on tech security
- Surveillance Report – Weekly roundup of privacy news

Articles & Research That Made an Impact

- "The Internet is a Surveillance Machine" – Bruce Schneier, *The Atlantic*
- "The Data Brokers Who Sell Your Identity" – *The New York Times*
- "You Are the Product" – *The Guardian* investigation into Facebook tracking
- "The World Is Watching" – *The Markup*'s analysis of facial recognition spread

Appendix D: A Final Reminder

Start where you are.

Use what you can.

And remember—you don't have to do everything to make a difference.

Every tool you install, every setting you change, every friend you help—that's a step toward a freer digital life.

Keep your tools sharp. Keep your circle informed.

And most of all: keep your choices intentional.

Glossary

Speak Privacy Fluently

This glossary is your cheat sheet. Whether you're brushing up or diving in for the first time, here's what you need to know—no jargon, no fluff, just clear definitions that stick.

Ad Tracking

The practice of monitoring users' online behavior to serve targeted advertisements. Trackers can follow clicks, scrolls, time spent on a page, and more—across websites and devices.

Algorithm

A set of rules or instructions a computer follows to solve a problem or make a decision. In privacy terms, algorithms decide what ads you see, what news shows up, and sometimes—who gets surveilled.

Authentication

The process of verifying that you are who you say you are. Common methods include passwords, fingerprint scans, and one-time codes. Two-factor authentication (2FA) adds an extra layer of protection.

Biometrics

Personal physical traits—like fingerprints, facial features, or voice patterns—used for identification. Biometrics can be convenient but are hard to change if compromised.

Browser Fingerprinting

A technique websites use to identify users based on their unique device settings—like screen size, fonts, and plugins—even without cookies.

Cookies

Small data files stored in your browser by websites you visit. Some cookies help with functionality (like staying logged in), while others track you for advertising.

Data Breach

An incident where personal or sensitive information is exposed without permission—often due to hacking, poor security, or insider leaks.

Data Broker

A company that collects, analyzes, and sells personal data—often without direct consent. They build profiles on individuals using public records, online activity, and purchase history.

Digital Footprint

The trail of data you leave behind when using the internet—like search queries, social media posts, device usage, and app activity.

Encryption

A method of scrambling data so only the intended recipient can read it. End-to-end encryption means even the service provider can't see your messages.

Facial Recognition

Technology that scans and identifies faces using algorithms. It's used in unlocking phones, law enforcement, and even marketing—often raising ethical and legal concerns.

IP Address

A unique number assigned to your device on a network, like a digital mailing address. Websites and services use it to identify your location or device.

Metadata

Data about data. For example, an email's metadata includes the sender, recipient, and time sent—but not the content. It reveals a lot, even without reading your messages.

Phishing

A scam tactic where attackers pretend to be trustworthy sources—like banks or services—to trick you into giving away personal info or passwords.

Privacy Settings

Controls you can adjust to limit who can see your information or track your activity. Found in browsers, apps, devices, and websites.

Private Browsing Mode

Also called Incognito Mode. It stops your browser from saving your history, cookies, and form data—but doesn't hide your activity from your internet provider or the websites you visit.

Surveillance Capitalism

A business model where companies extract, analyze, and sell personal data for profit—often without transparent consent. The term was popularized by scholar Shoshana Zuboff.

Tracking Pixel

A tiny invisible image embedded in emails or web pages to track if, when, and where content is viewed. Often used in marketing analytics.

Two-Factor Authentication (2FA)

An extra security step that combines something you know (like a password) with something you have (like a code sent to your phone).

Virtual Private Network (VPN)

A tool that encrypts your internet traffic and masks your location. It helps you browse more privately and access content securely—especially on public Wi-Fi.

Zero-Knowledge Encryption

A system where the service provider cannot access your encrypted data—because they literally don't have the key. This means only you can unlock it.

About the Author

V. Pathak is a digital privacy advocate, author, and entrepreneur with a deep passion for empowering everyday people to reclaim control over their personal data. He believes that privacy isn't just about hiding—it's about choosing how much of your life you share, with whom, and why.

With years of hands-on experience in technology, cybersecurity education, and real-world digital risk mitigation, Pathak has worked at the intersection of innovation and integrity. He's known for making complex privacy concepts feel human, relatable, and actionable—without ever dumbing them down.

His writing is grounded in personal conviction: that a free society depends on informed citizens, and that privacy is a basic right—not a luxury.

When he's not writing or consulting, Pathak actively researches global surveillance trends, emerging privacy tools, and the psychological effects of digital overexposure. He is an advocate for privacy-by-design technology and regularly contributes to thought leadership around ethical tech and digital dignity.

Above all, he is committed to helping readers, professionals, and communities feel less powerless in the face of algorithms, corporations, and government oversight.

Take Back Control is his call to action for anyone who wants to live connected, but not compromised.